The Kid's Guide to

Becoming the

BEST

You Can Be!

Developing 5 traits you need to achieve your personal best

Jill Frankel Hauser

Illustrations by Michael Kline

A WILLIAMSON *KIDS CAN!*® BOOK

WILLIAMSON BOOKS
NASHVILLE, TENNESSEE

Dedication

For Randy, my daily model of the principles that shaped this book.

ISBN-13: 978-0-8249-6789-5 (casebound)
ISBN-10: 0-8249-6789-5 (casebound)
ISBN-13: 978-0-8249-6788-8 (paper)
ISBN-10: 0-8249-6788-7 (paper)
Text copyright © 2006 by Jill Frankel Hauser
Illustrations copyright © 2006 by Michael Kline

Library of Congress Cataloging-in-Publication Data

Hauser, Jill Frankel, 1950-
   The kid's guide to becoming the best you can be : developing 5 traits you need to achieve your personal best /
Jill Frankel Hauser ; illustrations by Michael Kline.
      p. cm.
   "A Williamson kids can! book."
   Includes index.
   ISBN 0-8249-6789-5 (casebound : alk. paper) — ISBN 0-8249-6788-7 (pbk. : alk. paper)
   1. Children—Conduct of life—Juvenile literature. 2. Success in children—Juvenile literature. 3. Self-actualization
(Psychology) in children—Juvenile literature. I. Kline, Michael P. II. Title.
   BJ1631.H38 2006
   646.70083—dc22

                              2006015977

Photos used by permission:

page 16: Cesar E. Chavez ™/© 2006 The Cesar E. Chavez Foundation, www.chavezfoundation.org; **p. 21:** Lance Armstrong © Graham Watson Cycling Photography, www.grahamwatson.com; **page 28:** Brandon Keefe © BookEnds, www.bookends.org; **page 33:** top photo courtesy of Michael Cassara; bottom photo courtesy of Jill Frankel Hauser; **page 37:** Jourdan Urbach © Victor Urbach, Children Helping Children, www.childrenhelpingchildren.net ; **page 58:** Ryan Hreljac © Ryan's Well Foundation, www.ryanswell.ca; **page 73:** Craig Kielburger © Free The Children, www.freethechildren.com; **page 86:** Dr. Elisabeth Kalko © Daniel J. Splaine/The JASON Project, www.jason.org; **page 89:** Tim Berners-Lee © Le Fevre Communications; **page 106:** Chi Nguyen © Kim Nguyen, Viet Nam Youth Projects, www.vnyouthprojects.net; **page 118:** *Apollo 13* crew, NASA, scan by Ed Hengeveld; **page 122:** Martin Luther King, Jr., National Archives photo no. 306-SSM-4D(107)8, the Martin Luther King, Jr. Estate.

Kids Can!® series editor: **Susan Williamson**
Project editor: **Vicky Congdon**
Interior Design: **Sydney Wright**
Illustrations: **Michael Kline**

Published by Williamson Books
An imprint of Ideals Publications
535 Metroplex Drive, Suite 250
Nashville, TN 37211
(800) 586-2572

Printed and bound in China
All rights reserved.
10 9 8 7 6 5 4 3 2 1

Contents

BECOMING YOUR
Personal Best!

How would you like to be the best person you could possibly be, today and every day? You might be thinking, "Sure, who wouldn't, but how can I?" Well, for starters, you've picked up the right book. Being the best person you can be means leading a positive, productive life and making worthwhile and important contributions to the world around you. Achieving your personal best is not about what you own or how you look, but about who you are inside. It's about your *character*, the set of *traits* or special qualities you possess that make you who you are. This book will help you build several important character traits in fun and engaging ways.

DISCOVER THE FIVE KEY TRAITS

There are five essential character traits that make it possible to consistently be and do your best. The good news is that you can start building these traits today, in all kinds of ways both large and small. What's more, they are yours to keep for a lifetime!

Trait #1 **Making the most of who you are.** You believe in yourself, and you see yourself as a valuable person who has much to contribute, because you truly are.

Trait #2 **Getting involved.** You seize opportunities to be involved in positive, productive activities so that you're spending your time in meaningful ways that enrich your life.

Trait #3 **Doing the right thing.** You use your values and ideals to make thoughtful choices and to guide your actions.

Trait #4 **Going after knowledge.** You think the world is incredibly fascinating and full of amazing things to know, and you strive to learn all you can from it.

Trait #5 **Joining together.** You're ready to team up with others. You know how important it is to work well with other people — family, friends, classmates, and your community — to make the world a better place for all.

BUILD IMPORTANT SKILLS

In each chapter, you'll discover *why* it's important to make that particular trait part of your life. And you'll see *how*. To build each trait, you'll learn about five specific *character skills* you can develop and practice on your own.

You'll find real-life situations to consider that kids like you might face. What choices would you make? Reflect by writing in a journal. Or, use these dilemmas as springboards to start up a conversation about character with friends, family, or other adults. Pick an activity and give it a try. Then use the character skill you've practiced in your daily life and see how it works for you.

LOOK FOR EXCITING CHANGES!

Building these traits takes time. It's something exciting and important to work on throughout your life. (Adults do this, too!) But you'll also find that as soon as you start thinking about these five traits and begin developing the skills that support them, you'll notice some remarkable changes. You might find yourself getting along better with friends and family, and you may also make some new friends. Perhaps your grades will improve. You'll probably realize you're hardly ever bored because you're involved in so many exciting activities.

You may find you think more about your place in your community or view your community in a new way. You might even hear folks say, "What a great kid. Thanks for helping make the world a better place." When good things like these start to happen, you'll know you're on your way to becoming the best person you can be!

The adults in your life

It's important to have adults in your life who believe in you and encourage you to do your best. Perhaps one of those adults gave you this book! Young people live in all kinds of families. Maybe you live with your mom, dad, or both parents. Perhaps you live with your grandparents, adult brothers or sisters, or other relatives. Or, you might live with a foster parent or stepparent.

You likely have other adults in your life who don't live with you, but who also care about you, such as teachers, neighbors, coaches, or youth-group leaders. So think of the word "adult" as referring to any of the important grown-ups in your life. Share the ideas in this book with these special folks who want to help you do your best.

Making the Most

Imagine being able to make a difference within yourself and in the world — at home, at school, and in your community. Well, you can — when you have the trait of making the most of who you are. With this trait, you recognize and value your personal strengths and use them to become an awesome person. You know how to make the best use of all your special qualities and abilities — and that knowledge makes you capable of some truly amazing accomplishments!

Being this type of strong and effective person doesn't mean you have power to influence everything that happens to you. No one can have that. You can't control who's in your family, how other people behave, how much homework your teacher assigns, or if the track meet gets rained out. But you *can* control how you deal with what happens to you. *You* are in charge of your feelings and your actions.

This kind of personal power is not about pushing people around or having lots of cool stuff. That won't make you a better person or the world a better place. It's about how you treat others and what you have inside your heart and mind.

Successful people know how to use their best qualities and their special talents in the

# of Who You Are!

RECOGNIZING YOUR PERSONAL STRENGTHS AND USING THEM TO THE MAX!

most effective ways. You can make the most of the amazing person you are, too! Let's look at the skills it takes to develop this trait:

Confidence. It all starts with appreciating who you are and believing you can succeed.

Staying in control. Being able to handle your emotions means you always use responsible words and actions, even in tough or tricky situations.

Resilience. The ability to bounce back if things aren't going your way or something doesn't turn out the way you wanted keeps you from giving up.

Fitness. You can't make the most of everything you have to offer without respecting your mind *and* your body and feeling your best physically.

Purpose. You know you play an important part in making the world a better place.

Read on to find out more about these character skills so you can fully value who you are and get started on making the most of that special person!

Confidence

BELIEVING IN YOURSELF

Do you think you are important? Of course you are! Knowing you're a valuable person is the first step to believing in yourself. When you believe in yourself, you trust yourself to make good decisions, rather than just following the crowd. When you know you're important, you'll do what it takes to protect yourself — your mind, your body, your feelings — and stay healthy. When you're confident, you're willing to try new things and you won't be afraid to make a few mistakes. And when you respect yourself, other kids and adults will, too, and others won't be able to bully or boss you around.

Having this skill of *confidence* means you know who you are — and you like that person! *Don't* worry about being perfect — no one is. And being confident doesn't mean going around telling everyone how great you are — no one wants to hear someone brag. But do take time to quietly think about your abilities (what terrific things you can do) and your achievements (what terrific things you've accomplished). You'll realize what a valuable, important person you truly are.

Confidence means ... believing in yourself and knowing you're a valuable person.

Believing you can do it!

Confidence can change your life! Act as if you believe you'll succeed, and you'll discover that, most of the time, you do just fine. Let's say your teacher thinks your essay is awesome. She wants you to read it in front of the class, but you get *so* nervous when you have to speak in front of a lot of people. What would you do? Well, you might just say, "No thanks. I really don't want to," and let it go at that.

Or, you could try this "two steps to success" approach:
1. Talk yourself through it.
2. Then act as if you can do it!
It might go like this: "OK, I might be embarrassed, but I guess I can handle it. Other kids have read their essays and they're still alive. Hey, my writing must be pretty good if she wants me to read it. I guess I can give it a try!"

Think about how that confidence-building technique could help you handle these challenging situations:

* You want to take your skateboard down to the new skateboard park, but the kids hanging out there are really good and know lots of moves.
* You are invited to an event where you don't know anyone.
* Everyone in your class seems to understand the math skill the teacher is explaining, but you don't get it at all.

Now you try it!

Spend time reflecting on and appreciating the special person you are! See what happens when you …

* use one of your abilities (the great things you know how to do) to help out a friend or family member.
* describe a recent accomplishment (something great you've done) to a grandparent or other caring adult. They love sharing your pride!
* make a sketch or journal about yourself displaying your qualities (your positive beliefs, thoughts, and actions).
* master a new skill or technique in your favorite sport or hobby.

> "**W**hether you think you can or think you can't, you're right."
> —Henry Ford, automobile manufacturer

Package a unique product – YOU!

Advertisers really know how to sell their products. There's not a word or image in an ad that isn't focused on making you think that that particular product is the best ever! Use these same techniques to tell the world what a unique person you are. Redesign a cereal box, keeping the focus of every word and image on your message — how special you are!

What you need

- Scissors
- Construction or craft paper
- Empty cereal box
- Computer, markers, or colored pencils
- Photos (optional)
- Glue
- Small treasures or souvenirs

WHAT ARE THE *INGREDIENTS* THAT MAKE YOU WHO YOU ARE?

CHANGE THE *NUTRITION FACTS* TO A LIST OF *KEISHA FACTS*.

What you do

1 Cut paper to fit over each panel of the box. Using the style of the writing and images on the cereal box as inspiration, describe yourself in glowing terms. Write the text on your computer using bold or fancy fonts or use markers or colored pencils. Decorate with photos or drawings, or find clip art on the Internet.

2 Glue everything onto the panels and use them to cover the box. Use the box to hold small treasures that say something about you: souvenirs, ticket stubs, photos, jewelry you made, or a CD of a favorite song, for example.

DESIGN YOUR NAME AS A BANNER ACROSS THE FRONT.

Dealing with bullies

You have the right to feel safe all the time, and no one should take that right away from you. But that's just what bullies try to do. Bullies try to shake your confidence by making you feel scared, embarrassed, sad, and stressed. Remember: It's not your fault if you are being harassed. It's the bully who's got problems.

Bullies might pick on a kid for no reason at all, but usually they look for someone they think won't stand up for himself. Or, they find someone who gets upset easily and reacts in a big way to their teasing. Here are some tips to keep a bully from thinking you are that kind of kid.

Be confident. Sometimes acting brave (even if you have to pretend) actually gives you courage, and holding your head high might do just enough to keep a bully away.

Keep your cool. *Ignoring* bullies keeps them from getting the power over you they want. It's no fun for them if you don't even notice their teasing. So try not to react to their meanness and just walk away.

If paying no attention doesn't stop the bully, try *a good comeback.* Look the bully in the eye, stay cool, and make a quick, to-the-point comeback, such as "You can't be talking to me!" or "whatever." Then walk away. (Important: If you think the bully might become violent, go straight to an adult instead.)

And of course, *don't be a bully back.* Fighting or using bad words will only get you in trouble. What's more, it will show the bully that he really can control your actions.

Take a stand, together. *Use a buddy system* where kids tell the bully to stop the teasing, then walk away together.

Report the bully. If you can't stop the bully on your own, you must *tell a parent or teachers or other adults at school.* If you're afraid that reporting a bully will only make the situation worse, be sure the adults understand that, too. You'll not only help yourself, you'll be protecting others from being future bully targets.

> "**Y**ou have to have confidence in your ability, and then be tough enough to follow through."
> —Rosalynn Carter, former First Lady

Staying in Control

MANAGING YOUR WORDS AND ACTIONS

Are you in charge of yourself and your behavior? You can be! Of course, you aren't in control of everything that happens to you. Your mom's car might break down when you had hoped she could take you to the mall. You might not get invited to a party even though all your friends are going. A friend borrowed a favorite shirt and now there's a big spot on the front. And you can't always control how you feel in response to those situations. What you *are* in charge of is your reactions — what you say and do. Do you get angry and maybe act in a way that you later regret? Or do you feel disappointed (understandably!), but then let go of it and move on? No one can make you feel or do anything. How you respond is up to you.

When everything goes your way, it's easy! When your team wins, it's fun to show the world how happy you are. But if your team loses, you probably feel really disappointed. Do you let yourself get angry and show your feelings by screaming bad words at the other team or their fans? Or would you say to yourself or to your friends, "This is a big disappointment, but we've got another chance to win next week." It's these kinds of tricky situations that challenge you to behave in a way that shows you have the skill of *staying in control*.

Sometimes you can plan your actions so that things will more likely go your way. You can't control the grade you get on your history test or whether you get a part in the school musical. But if you listen in class and study at home, you'll increase your chances of doing well on the test. If you study the script and learn the songs, you're more likely to get a part in the musical.

So don't just *have* a good day. *Make it* a good day by taking the time to think things over and stay in control before you "take action." You'll likely make it a good day for everyone around you, too!

The "keeping your cool" plan

1. Understand the problem. Be aware of situations that trigger negative feelings.

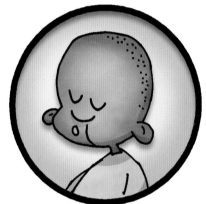

2. Calm down. Count to 10 and take some slow, deep breaths.

3. Brainstorm choices. Think of positive ways to react.

4. Do the right thing. Do what's best for everyone involved and make sure no one gets hurt, by either words or actions.

The plan in action

This handy four-step plan works when you need to act quickly. For example, let's say a kid makes fun of you because you wear glasses, "Hey, four eyes!" You …

1. Understand the problem. Think, *that was a rude remark. It makes me angry.*

2. Calm down. *I'll relax and take a few slow deep breaths.*

3. Brainstorm choices. *I could try these comebacks: "How boring. Can't you think of something new?" … "Grow up" … "Ouch, that really hurt" … "So sorry you've got only two."*

4. Do the right thing. *I'll choose one of the above comebacks — they all make the point without me overreacting. Then I'll walk away.*

The plan also works when you have more time to think about the situation. What if you don't make it onto the track team? You …

1. Understand the problem. Think, *I really wanted to be on that team. I did my very best at the tryouts. I feel so disappointed.*

2. Calm down. *I'll go for a bike ride to work off some of the bad feelings while I think things over.*

3. Brainstorm choices. *I could: Complain to the coach. Ask the coach how I can get on the team next semester. Give up and be miserable. Go out for another sport. Jog every day and improve my time.*

4. Do the right thing. *I'll ask the coach what I can do to make it onto the team next semester and I'll follow her plan. I'll let her know I'm interested in case someone drops out. And I'll keep in shape so I'm ready!*

> **"You** have no control over what the other guy does. You only have control over what you do."
> —A. J. Kitt, World Cup skier and Olympic athlete

KEEP-YOUR-COOL BRACELET

Make a four-bead bracelet to remind you of the four steps of THE "KEEPING YOUR COOL" PLAN (see pages 13–14). Touch each bead as you think through the steps.

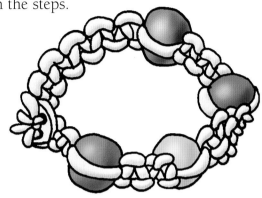

What you need

- 2 strands of hemp cord, 60" (1.5 m) and 30" (75 cm)
- Push pin or tape
- Stiff cardboard
- 4 colored beads: indigo, blue, yellow, and red
- Button with four holes

What you do

1 Fold the two strands in half and, holding them together, tie a single knot to form a loop as shown. You now have four strands. Using the push pin or tape, attach the loop to the cardboard to hold the loop in place. Place the two shorter strands in the middle.

LONG CORD
SHORT CORD

2 Follow the three steps on the right to make several knots, each time starting the knot on a different side.

◀ PLACE THE LEFT OUTSIDE STRAND OVER THE MIDDLE TWO STRANDS AND UNDER THE RIGHT OUTSIDE STRAND.

◀ PLACE THE RIGHT OUTSIDE STRAND UNDER THE MIDDLE STRANDS AND UP THROUGH THE LOOP YOU JUST MADE.

◀ PULL THE OUTSIDE STRANDS TIGHT TO TIE THE KNOT.

3 Slip the indigo bead onto the middle two strands. Tie a knot to hold it in place.

4 Repeat steps 2 and 3 to add the remaining beads in this order: blue, yellow, and red. Tie several additional knots.

5 End your bracelet by slipping one strand through each hole of the button. Knot the end of each strand and trim.

6 Slip the button through the loop to secure the bracelet.

Why those four bead colors?

Many people believe that certain colors can affect our emotions and influence our actions. Indigo represents wisdom; blue represents calmness; yellow represents good decision-making skills; and red represents action and confidence. Let the power of color help you put the four-step plan into action!

Cesar Chavez:
Thoughtful reactions created positive change!

Cesar E. Chavez led many marches in support of farm workers and their struggles for better working conditions. Here he is marching with the Canadian Labor Leaders in Toronto.

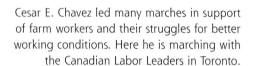

"**N**onviolence in action is a very potent force and it can't be stopped."
—Cesar Chavez

Cesar Chavez (SHAH-vez) could have been an angry man. Cesar's family lost its farm in Arizona when he was a child. His family became *migrant* farm workers (they traveled from farm to farm to harvest crops). Cesar attended more than 30 schools, and then left school after eighth grade to work fulltime in the fields. Life was harsh for the migrant workers, and they were very poor.

Cesar knew that if workers got angry and fought violently for change, lives would be lost. In addition, people would not respect the farm workers. So Cesar and the workers controlled their anger. They joined together to let the world know of the hardships and injustices they faced. Cesar founded the National Farm Workers Association, which later became the United Farm Workers of America (UFW). The UFW was America's first farm workers' *union* (an organization of workers that promotes better conditions). The UFW called *strikes* (the workers walked off the job to protest the working conditions) and *boycotts* (people were asked not to buy California grapes, wine, and lettuce to show their support for the migrant workers). And Cesar *fasted*, when he didn't eat for many days to bring attention to his cause. These actions were all powerful, yet peaceful ways of demanding better and fair treatment.

Thanks to Cesar's leadership, growers agreed to work with the UFW to improve conditions. Cesar had a confident motto — *si se puede* (it can be done). And he did it through controlled and peaceful actions.

Resilience

YOU CAN BOUNCE BACK, READY TO TRY AGAIN

Stretch out a rubber band as far as you can. Let it fly across an empty room. Now find it and look closely. It's in perfect shape after that challenging (for a rubber band!) experience — in fact, it's ready for another flight. Now that's *resilience*.

People can have challenging experiences, too. Troubles … setbacks … mistakes … ! Not everyone deals with problems the same way. Some people get down on themselves. They give up. They don't want to try again. But successful people are as resilient as that rubber band! They don't let setbacks get in their way. They stay positive and give it another try. In fact, successful people even take time to try to figure out what went wrong and why. They think, "This didn't work out … yet. So I'll try something different next time!" To see how you can be as resilient as that rubber band, read on!

Resilience means … being able to recover from setbacks and disappointments.

Bouncing right back!

Everyone faces difficult situations at times. It's how we handle them that makes the difference. Resilience helps you make a quick recovery and keeps bad experiences from getting you down. Say kids laugh at you for not understanding a joke because English is not your first language. What would you do? You might walk away embarrassed, vowing to never say anything when you are with groups of kids. Or, you could bounce right back and join in on the fun. Tell the kids if they explain the joke, you'll share one in Cantonese and explain it to them!

Changing an embarrassing situation into a funny one is one way to stretch and strengthen your resilience. You might also try to find something positive about a negative or disappointing event or look for an important lesson to take away from an experience that doesn't go quite right. And remember, resilience goes a long way but it can't solve every problem. If your worries are too big to handle on your own, seek out someone you can trust (a parent, teacher, or faith or community group leader) and ask for help.

Think about how those bounce-back behaviors could keep your spirits up when you face situations like these:

* You think kids are gossiping about you.
* Your parents are always arguing.
* You receive a disappointing grade on a test.

Now you try it!

When something doesn't go quite right, see what happens when you …

* have an optimistic attitude.
* break a big goal down into small steps.
* hang out with positive people who cheer you up and encourage you.
* get involved in rewarding activities, such as sports, art, music, clubs, or volunteer work.
* are your own best friend. When something doesn't go quite right for you, let that little voice in your head remind you why you are such a great person.

"My resilience comes from wanting to be a happy person — everything I do is always about trying to find a solution."

—Dan O'Brien, gold medalist in the decathlon, 1996 Olympics

MAKE SUPER-RESILIENT FLUBBER!

Mix up a batch of flubber and see what real resilience looks like! You can stretch it! You can push it, prod it, and mold it back into its original shape. Flubber bounces back when you drop it. You can even press it onto a newspaper comic strip and pick up the picture.

> "**H**e's a million rubber bands in his resilience."
> —Alan K. Simpson, senator

What you need

- 2 mixing bowls
- Mixing spoon
- Water, 1 cup (250 ml)
- White glue, ½ cup (125 ml)
- Borax
- Measuring spoons
- Ziplock plastic bag for storage

What you do

1 In one bowl, mix half the water and the white glue.

2 In the second bowl, mix half the water and the borax. You might like your flubber firm and bouncy or slimy and stretchy. Experiment with the amount of borax, using anywhere from 1 to 2 teaspoons (5 to 10 ml) up to 2 tablespoons (25 ml).

3 Stir the borax mixture while adding the glue mixture to it.

Have a friend who's going through a tough time?

Now you know how to help him be resilient!

- ✓ Invite him to do things with you (sports, clubs, eat lunch).
- ✓ Tell your friend why you think she is a great person and why you value her friendship.
- ✓ Relate a diffcult experience you had and how you pulled through.
- ✓ Encourage him to keep trying. Ask how you can help.
- ✓ Be a good listener and offer encouragement.
- ✓ If your friend's worries are too big for her to handle, encourage her to seek out an adult she trusts for help.

Fitness

TAKING CARE OF YOUR BODY AND MIND

Being fit is an important part of being the best you can be. Why? When you are fit, you are more able to enjoy life to the fullest. A healthy body gives you the energy to do things you love to do.

How do *you* score on this fitness checklist?

When *fitness* is a regular part of your life, you:

* eat healthy food.
* are active and get plenty of exercise.
* get enough sleep.
* know how to relax and "de-stress" when necessary.

When you take care of yourself in these ways, your body feels great. And when your body feels great, your mind does, too. You're more likely to be in a good mood and be ready to take on whatever comes your way. Didn't do so well on the checklist above? Not to worry! It's not hard to make small changes in your behavior that will have you feeling better. Staying fit and healthy will help you have a terrific day!

So there I was in left field, and I hear the crack of the bat. I looked up and could see this baseball ...

And I was wondering why it kept getting bigger, and bigger, and bigger.

And then it hit me ...

Fitness means ...
keeping your body at its personal best.

20 BECOMING THE BEST YOU CAN BE!

Lance Armstrong: Be fit. Live strong.

Lance Armstrong heads toward the finish line to win his seventh consecutive Tour de France, a world-famous bike race of more than 2,000 miles (3,220 km).

Most kids use their bikes as a handy way to get around. But for Lance Armstrong, cycling was a way to become a great athlete and achieve his personal best. Lance had a passion for fitness. As a kid, he was determined to do his best on the swim team. He rode his bike 10 miles (16 km) to the pool to practice at 5:30 A.M. Then he rode to school. After school it was back to the pool, then back home. He was logging in 20 miles (32 km) on the bike and 6 miles (9.6 km) in the pool every day!

During high school, it became clear that Lance was most talented as a bicycle racer. He left high school to train with the Junior National Cycling Team (he graduated from a private academy the following year). He went on to achieve great wins and disappointing losses, but the losses only spurred him to keep on training.

At 25, Lance was diagnosed with a serious form of cancer. He took time from cycling for treatment. A disease that would have weakened most people only made Lance determined to train hard and regain his strength. He is famous for winning the Tour de France (a grueling bicycle race) an amazing seven times in a row!

Lance founded the Lance Armstrong Foundation. His yellow Livestrong wristbands have helped the foundation raise more than $9 million for cancer research. Perhaps Lance's greatest achievement is the inspiration he has given to others. He fought back against a life-threatening disease to become a cycling superstar!

"I will be riding a bike in 10 years time because I feel better when I do exercise and I want to enjoy true good health."
—Lance Armstrong

Four steps to fitness!

1. Follow healthy eating habits. Adults probably buy the food and make most of the meals at home. But you can make food choices, too.

* Eat a variety of foods to make sure your body gets all the nutrients you need.
* Be sure to eat several servings of fruits and vegetables every day (face it, you'll *never* stop hearing that one because it really is important!).
* Make healthy choices like water, milk, or pure juice instead of soda pop or punch (they're loaded with sugar and don't give you any nutrients).
* Read labels. Does that bag of snack food give you any protein, vitamins, or fiber or is it mostly fat, sugar, chemicals, and salt?
* Be adventurous — you may discover a healthy food that becomes your new favorite!

2. Be active. Find ways to exercise every day if possible or at least several times a week. You may love swimming, track, or softball. But sports aren't the only way to keep your body moving. Maybe you enjoy dancing, karate, or bouncing on a trampoline. Walking your dog or bicycling to your friend's house counts for physical activity, too. Brainstorm a list of active, fun alternatives to sitting in front of a television or computer screen. Encourage your whole family or your friends to "get up and go" with you!

3. Remember to relax. Being a kid means you are busy. You have a long school day. You have homework. Then come chores. Maybe you practice a sport or a musical instrument. *Phew!* You need time to de-stress! Violent movies and TV shows will not calm you down. Instead, fill your mind with positive thoughts. Try sketching in an art pad while you listen to music. Relax in

your room as you read a book or magazine or write an entry in your journal. Keep a handful of modeling clay to mold in a ziplock bag in your backpack. Exercise is one of the very best ways to de-stress, so try some of the Be Active ideas on page 22. Be sure to make time for relaxing activities you enjoy.

4. Get enough sleep. All living things need sleep to survive — and that includes you! Not getting enough sleep can make you feel groggy, grumpy, and even clumsy. More important, lack of sleep can hurt your immune system, which is important for keeping you from getting sick. Sleep also recharges your brain and helps you be more alert and able to learn. Most experts think that kids need about 10 hours of sleep each night. So although it's annoying to hear, "Head up to bed please!" right in the middle of a TV show, it's just what you need to do to feel great and be your best tomorrow!

Now you try it!

See what happens when you …

* get one more hour of sleep a night.
* eat a piece of fresh fruit at each meal.
* exercise for 20 minutes every day for a week.
* take 15 minutes a day to relax.
* share a positive idea or a happy ending from a book or movie with family or friends.

Pyramid Power!

Use the nutrition pyramid from the U. S. Department of Agriculture to help you make healthy food choices and to make sure you eat a balanced diet. There may be one posted in your cafeteria and you can download your own copy at **www.myPyramid.gov**. See page 124 for other nutrition resources.

FUN FITNESS FOODS

You've heard it again and again, "Eat your fruits and vegetables!" Here are some fun ways to fill your body with nutrients from healthy foods. The recipes are best when you add your own personal touch and make them your way with favorite ingredients. After all, you're the chef *and* the diner!

"Eat the Bowl Too" Salad

You can enjoy fresh veggies anytime, anywhere. And don't forget to munch on the bowl!

What you need

- Salad dressing of your choice
- Green, yellow, or red pepper, cut in half and seeds removed
- Knife
- Carrots
- Celery stalks

What you do

1 Place a dollop of dressing in the bottom of one pepper half.

2 Slice the carrot, celery, and the other pepper half into short, thin dipping sticks (ask for adult help). Place the cut veggies in the "pepper" bowl.

3 Now enjoy your on-the-go veggie treat!

 **You're the Chef!**

Fill the bowl with any kind of small, sturdy veggies: broccoli or cauliflower florets, jicama, radishes, cucumber, or cherry tomatoes.

Use your favorite thick dip: guacamole, hummus, yogurt raita, or any creamy salad dressing.

Fill the pepper bowl with coleslaw or a small salad. Eat with a fork.

Hey Mom, the next time you're at the store, would you pick up some jicama, hummus, and yogurt raita?

Fabulous Fruit Smoothie

There are so many ways to make a super smoothie — and all of them are super simple!

What you need
- Low-fat yogurt, 1 cup (250 ml)
- Frozen banana, cut into chunks
- Blender

What you do

Process all the ingredients in a blender just until smooth. Serve right away.

You're the Chef!

- Use any flavor of yogurt.
- Use juice or milk instead of yogurt.
- Use almost any kind of fruit: berries, melon, pineapple, mango, even leftover fruit salad.
- Add fruit juice or milk to get the blender moving and a thinner smoothie.
- Freeze the fruit to make the smoothie smoothi-er.
- Keep chunks of overripe banana in a ziplock bag in the freezer. You'll always be ready to make a smoothie!

FIT KIT

What's in *your* Fit Kit? Anything that helps you get moving! Here are some ideas.

Music CDs or MP3 files. Pick songs you can jump rope, jog in place, or dance to.

Water bottle. Decorate one with permanent markers.

Fitness wear. Personalize a T-shirt, sweatbands, and socks with fabric paint.

Jump rope. Perfect for an indoor or outdoor workout anywhere, anytime!

Sense of Purpose
MAKING A DIFFERENCE

Sense of purpose means ... pursuing goals that will make a difference and making worthwhile contributions to the world around you.

Do you ever think about how you can make your life important? Or what contributions you'd like to make? These are huge questions that adults ponder, too. Take a survey. Pose these questions to your parents, teachers, community- and youth-group leaders, and your friends. From many people, you'll likely get this answer, "Our lives are most important when we help make the world a better place."

Everyone has a part, big or small. Whether you are the leader of a country or you walk your neighbor's dog, you can help others and improve the world around you. When you have a *sense of purpose* and you try to carry it out, you are making the most of who you are. Having a sense of purpose is powerful because with it one person — you! — can make a difference!

Figuring out your part

Making the world a better place is an awesome purpose — but it feels like such a big one. How can one person make a difference? Start by asking yourself: What do I believe in? What is important to me? What can I do to make what I believe in and what's important to me happen? Maybe you believe that if people were just a little more thoughtful and helpful to others, life would be better for everyone. Put that belief into action!

Your mom loves to garden, but she never seems to have the time on the weekends to finish all her projects. One Saturday afternoon, you notice she is outside weeding the front flower bed. Then she gets a phone call. She lets you know she's going to pick up your sister from softball practice. Before she drives off, you hear her say, "I'll *never* get those flowers planted before dark!" You realize that her round trip to the softball field and back is just enough time to finish the weeding and get the last of the flowers planted. You get to work. You mom returns, jumps out of the car, and breaks into a big smile when she sees that front bed! You've certainly helped make *her* world a better place! See how easy it is to get started?

You can make a difference in big and small ways. How could you show that in these situations?

* Your dad has a meeting at your school. He usually cleans up the kitchen right after dinner, but he had to leave it a mess and rush out to make it to the meeting on time.
* Your town has organized a "Clean Up the Park Day." Volunteers are needed, but the signup sheets you've seen around town are looking pretty empty.
* You think it would be cool to be a geologist and study the Earth when you grow up. You wonder what you could be doing now to achieve your goal.

> **"S**ome men see things as they are and say, 'Why?' I dream of things that never were and say, 'Why not?'"
> —George Bernard Shaw, playwright

Now you try it!

See what happens when you ...

* do something extraordinary for your family, like cook a special meal or make everyone's bag lunch on a Thursday night.
* offer to help your neighbor set up for her yard sale and ask if she could use your help waiting on customers.
* offer to be a "greeter" and welcome new students to your school.

Brandon Keefe's purpose: creating libraries for kids!

Brandon Keefe's book-collection drives have helped young readers all over the world. He traveled to India in the summer of 2005 to help with a library there.

> **"**It's great to know you've made a difference and things are going to change because of what you've done."
> —Brandon Keefe

"My heroes are the ones who understand there's a need and really take action to eradicate the problem instead of just sitting back and thinking about it," said Brandon Keefe. That must make Brandon a hero himself.

When he was only eight years old, Brandon visited Hollygrove Children's Home in California. It was a place with lots of kids, but no books. Suddenly he had a brainstorm. What about all those books he had outgrown? His friends must have lots, too. He could collect books and donate them to Hollygrove to create a library. Brandon's sense of purpose spread. Soon he had more than 800 books. Retired librarians offered to organize them. The Junior League of Los Angeles donated the furniture and decorated. The Hollygrove library was born.

As a seventh grader, Brandon suggested a book drive as a community service project for his middle school. In one week, he and his fellow students collected 7,000 books! These became a new library for a local public school. Next Brandon set up BookEnds, a nonprofit organization that has since collected tens of thousands of books, completed dozens of libraries, and helped thousands of kids who didn't have access to books. But the best part is that Brandon's organization has given other kids a sense of purpose. BookEnds teaches kids how to hold their own book-collection drives!

VOLUNTEER!

If you think one ordinary kid can't make a difference, read about Brandon Keefe (see left), Ryan Hreljac (see page 58), Craig Kielburger (see page 73), and Chi Nguyen (see page 106). Opportunities to make the world a better place are all around you, right in your community. Get your whole family involved. Have your friends and classmates join in, too. Here are a few ideas to get you started.

"The purpose of life is to live a life of purpose."
—Richard Leider, author and motivational speaker

Share Your Skills

Think about what you can do to help others:
- Read books
- Tutor kids
- Teach computer skills
- Gardening
- Pet care
- Music lessons
- Sports coach

For an awesome way to let others know what you and your friends can do and that you're ready to help, see CREATE A KIDS' YELLOW PAGES, page 90.

Contribute to Your Community

Chances are, the places on this list could use your help! Ask an adult to help you contact them to find out what a kid your age with your skills could do. Then, volunteer your time, either by yourself, or with your family or as part of a youth or community group.

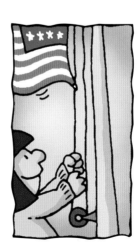

- Schools
- Museums
- Convalescent homes
- Senior centers
- Hospitals
- Libraries
- Animal shelters
- Food shelf

For other ideas on community service, see CITIZENSHIP, pages 120–123 and RESOURCES, page 124. You'll learn more about the power of purpose and the benefit of spending your time on issues and activities that are meaningful to you in the next chapter, GETTING INVOLVED!

Trait #2

Getting

What are your favorite ways to spend your time? Probably some of them are just plain fun or relaxing, such as listening to music or hanging out with friends. But does your life also include plenty of "productive activities"? You know, the ones that make you a better person or make the world a better place — things like practicing an instrument, joining in sports, volunteering, homework, chores, or being a member of a school club? (It's not that these activities aren't fun, too. They just take a bit more effort and commitment.) When you pursue activities like these, you have the trait of getting involved — with your family, your friends, your school, and your community. And that means you know how to make the best use of your time!

What character skills does it take to be a person who's eager to dive in and get involved?

Initiative. Not only can you come up with an idea or goal for something you'd like to do or accomplish but — more important — you're ready to take that all-important first step. Ideas are a great place to start, but not if they just stay inside your head!

Focus. You can keep your "eye on the prize," and you don't let yourself get distracted from the goal you want to accomplish or the activity you

Involved!

SPENDING YOUR TIME IN REWARDING WAYS

want to pursue, even if it means there are other things along the way that you may not be able to do. What's more, you're willing to put in time and effort to accomplish your goal.

Perseverance. You can stick with a plan to reach your goal even when the going gets tough (and frankly, it sometimes does).

Creativity. You can see things in new ways and come up with fresh ideas to produce something original. This kind of creative thinking can help to get you smoothly over any bumps in the road and have a lot of fun challenging yourself, too.

Resourcefulness. You see the exciting possibilities around you and use these opportunities to get you closer to your goal.

Ready to try some fun ways to put these character skills into action? Not only will you get to spend more time doing and learning about things that really interest and excite you, but you'll find that this "getting involved" attitude spreads to other activities that you might not know so well or that might be more challenging. And, quite simply, spending your time pursuing worthwhile activities helps you become a more productive and more interesting person. You can see why it's a key trait in becoming the best you can be!

Initiative

MAKING THINGS HAPPEN

"The secret of getting ahead is getting started. The secret of getting started is breaking your complex overwhelming tasks into small manageable tasks, and then starting on the first one."

—Mark Twain, author

Initiative is that first spark that gets things going. It's what moves things from the "idea stage" to the "action stage." What do you want to accomplish? Become? Create? Make better? Nothing can happen without initiative.

This character skill helps you get going on smaller tasks like straightening up your room, walking your dog every day, or practicing over the weekend for the upcoming spelling bee. It also helps you take the first steps toward accomplishing bigger goals like becoming a member of the swim team, starting a skateboarding club, or making sure the library offers a super CD collection for kids. Sometimes tasks and goals seem overwhelming. But if you just focus on taking that first step, no matter how small, you'll be on the right path for getting the job done or accomplishing your goal.

No one can do it for you. It's up to you. That's why you often hear that the first step is the most difficult. Only *you* can take the initiative to make things happen for you!

> **Initiative means ...**
> starting toward a goal or carrying out a plan all on your own.

If you're an American whose ancestors were originally from Europe, they may have come to the U.S. in the great wave of immigration in the early 1900s. Onorio Grieco and Catarina Giannetti entered the U.S. through Ellis Island around 1905. Their family of first-generation Italian Americans was born in Brooklyn, New York.

Immigrants show initiative!

Hundreds of years ago, people left their homes in Europe to live in North America thousands of miles (km) away. Their voyage across the ocean was so dangerous that many didn't survive. Yet people continued to journey to this "land of opportunity," and from 1892 to 1954, 12 million immigrants entered the United States through the federal immigration station on Ellis Island, New York. Even now, every day, hundreds of people from all over the world leave their homes behind. Immigrants travel by boat, car, train, and plane to start new lives around the globe because someone has the initiative to pursue the idea that "Life will be better there for our family."

The immigrant spirit is a powerful force that shapes our world. People who take action to better their lives and the lives of their families are taking that all-important first step in a journey to make dreams come true. Who took the initiative to bring your family to where you live now? What if no one had taken that first step — how would your life be different today?

> "**A** journey of a thousand miles begins with a single step."
> —Lao-tsu, philosopher

America continues to be a nation shaped by the diverse cultures of the immigrants who settle here to create a new life for themselves and their families.

Taking the initiative!

You love to draw and you'd really like to get better at it. You're curious about that after-school drawing club. The next meeting is coming up, but you don't think you'll know anyone, so you're feeling shy about attending. It's so much easier to just keep walking past that sign-up sheet in the front lobby. But the artwork has been on display right next to it and it's awesome! You want to draw like that!

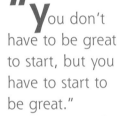

"**Y**ou don't have to be great to start, but you have to start to be great."
—Zig Ziglar, author

Remember, using the character skill of initiative means getting from the idea stage (wishing you could draw better) to the action stage (doing something to make your drawing better!). How about inviting a friend to go with you to the upcoming meeting? Or, compliment one of the kids whose artwork is on display and ask if you can come along to the next meeting with her. You might also check in with the teacher. Let her know you're interested and show her some of your sketches. Find out what's planned for the next meeting so you can arrive with some ideas in mind. It's probably not so hard to think of putting your name on that sign-up sheet now, is it?

Think about ways a spark of initiative could change these other situations:

* Wherever you turn, you and your friends see "No Skateboarding" signs. Why can't kids have a place to skateboard?
* You want to join the track team, but you feel out of shape.
* Your family keeps talking about having a barbecue at the lake but it never happens.

Now you try it!

See what happens when you …

* get to soccer practice a few minutes early so you can work on that maneuver you've been having trouble with.
* start homework within an hour of getting home from school.
* clean your room before being asked.
* start reviewing for a quiz the day it's announced instead of the night before it's scheduled.

DREAM, THEN DO!

Do you think about your big goals in life? Then do you wonder how you could ever achieve them? Remember, every goal has a place to begin. Writing down what you need to get done to accomplish a goal can help you see where to start (which is often the hardest part). And it's easier to take the initiative to accomplish a series of small steps.

So, think about a dream you have and identify the small but important first step toward getting you there. And then list the next step, and the next … hey, you're on your way!

"Whatever you do, or dream you can, begin it."
—Johann Wolfgang von Goethe, author

What you need
- Sheet of paper
- Thin markers or colored pencils

What you do

1 Fold the paper in half so it looks like a tall greeting card.

2 Show your dream or goal on the cover.

3 On the inside, write each step you'll need to take to achieve your goal. Check off each step as you complete it.

Focus

PUTTING EFFORT INTO WHAT YOU REALLY WANT

When you want to see an object in the distance, you reach for the binoculars and bring it into focus. It quickly goes from being a fuzzy, far-off thing to something you can see sharply and clearly. Well, it works just the same way with a goal. Think of your time and effort as your "binoculars" — when you apply them to something you really want to achieve, your goal becomes clearer and you can see smaller details. Whether it's learning to skate backward or acing tomorrow's geography test, centering all your energy and concentration on your goal will really help you to pull it off.

> **Focus means ...** concentrating effort on a goal without getting distracted.

You have to make some choices, however. It would be great if we could do absolutely everything we'd like to do and do it all exceptionally well. But we'd have to be super-human! Having the skill of *focus* helps you figure out, then carry out, what's most important among all the things that are demanding your attention. Imagine learning how to concentrate your time and effort on something without letting anything else get in your way, and you'll see that focus is a powerful force for accomplishing a goal or getting really good at something you want to learn how to do. So, let's see how to sharpen that focus!

Jourdan Urbach:

Amazing focus creates amazing music!

Jourdan Urbach performs the "Wieniawski Violin Concerto" at his benefit concert for the Houston Chapter of the National Multiple Sclerosis Society.

How do you get ready for a solo performance at Lincoln Center for the Performing Arts in New York when you are 11 years old? That was the challenge for Jourdan Urbach, who took up the violin when he was almost three years old. Focus was the answer. Jourdan practices three hours every day, takes lessons, and attends many rehearsals. This incredible focus on his music has made Jourdan an amazing concert violinist.

Jourdan has performed on *Good Morning America, CNN,* and *The Today Show* and at Madison Square Garden and has been featured in *The New York Times* and *People* magazine. At age 13, he made his debut on the main stage at Carnegie Hall in New York. One of his most rewarding places to perform, however, is in hospital pediatric wards. When he was in elementary school, Jourdan was fascinated by a book by Dr. Fred Epstein, a pediatric neurosurgeon. He met with the doctor and asked how he could help the sick children at Beth Israel Medical Center, where Dr. Epstein practices. That conversation led to Jourdan founding a charity organization, Children Helping Children. He has since raised over $200,000 for medical research and national medical charities through benefit concerts.

And music is not the only area in which Jourdan is able to focus his talents. At age 11, his first novel was published, followed by a second one, *Inside the Music,* two years later.

Jourdan's goal is to become a neurosurgeon. With his laser-sharp focus, Jourdan will certainly achieve his dreams.

> "If you keep your eyes open in life and follow your passions, you can do great things."
> —Jourdan Urbach

Focus, then action!

Your dad asks you to clean your room before your soccer game. Not a bad idea, because somewhere under all that mess is your soccer uniform. But you sit frozen on your bed. It seems like an impossible task with piles of papers here, food wrappers there, and heaps of clothing everywhere. And you need to leave in 45 minutes!

No problem! Just concentrate your efforts and zero in on each "disaster zone" at a time. First, throw away all trash (that's an easy place to start). Next, gather all clothes, then sort them (clean or dirty). Hey, there's your soccer uniform! Now make piles of school papers and books. Wow, your room is starting to look like a nice place to hang out! And you're ready to leave on time.

In these situations, how could you focus your efforts on solving the problem?

* You agreed to help your dad organize all the sports equipment in the garage but your favorite TV program comes on soon.
* You come out of a daydream and hear your teacher say, "So, finish up those other math problems the way we just did this one."
* You'd like to display your awesome collection of geodes but the shelves in your room are too cluttered with stuff you never use.

Now you try it!

See what happens when you …

* start a collection that focuses on one type of thing: heart-shaped rocks, sports cards, pencil toppers, or key chains.
* develop one new skill in a favorite activity, such as sketching a realistic version of your favorite animal or learning a new skateboard maneuver.
* tackle your weekend chores first thing on Saturday and finish them before you get distracted by anything else.

SHARPEN-YOUR-FOCUS VIEWER

Build this viewer to celebrate the power of sharp focus. Forcing light through a pinhole focuses it into an amazing image. Focusing your energy on a goal results in an amazing accomplishment!

What you need

- Marker
- Ruler
- Clean empty chip can with plastic lid (transluent if possible)
- Wax paper or tissue paper (if the lid is clear)
- Utility knife (for adult use only)
- Push pin
- Masking tape
- Aluminum foil or dark construction paper
- Scissors

What you do

1 Draw a line about 2" (5 cm) up from the bottom of the can. Ask an adult to use the utility knife to cut the can into two pieces along that line.

2 Use the push pin to make a hole in the center of the metal end of the shorter piece.

3 Place the plastic lid onto the open end of the shorter piece (if the lid is clear, insert a piece of wax paper or tissue paper first). With the masking tape, connect the parts as shown.

4 The inside of the can must be dark, so wrap the can with foil or dark construction paper, sealing the edges with tape. Tuck in the foil or paper at the top. On a bright day, hold the viewer right up to your face and cup your hands around the open end. Shut one eye and look through the open end with your other eye. Check out the pictures on the plastic "screen."

How does the viewer work?

We see an object when light reflects off it and into our eyes. The viewer's pinhole acts as a lens, forcing the light reflecting off the object you are viewing through the hole to form a small image on the plastic lid. The image is dim, but focused. Light travels in straight lines so it flips the image as it passes through the tiny hole.

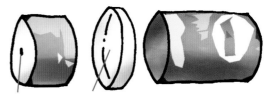

PINHOLE   PLASTIC LID

Perseverance

STICKING TO YOUR GOALS

Perseverance means ... working steadily to accomplish a goal, even when there are setbacks.

Perseverance is the steady action or "I won't give up attitude" that keeps you moving toward your goals. It may not always be easy, but you hang in there. If that sounds like hard work, well, often it is! But that doesn't mean it's not fun or satisfying or rewarding. Think of the pleasure a runner gets from completing a marathon after months of training. Imagine a writer's feeling of satisfaction when he writes the final sentence of the story he's been working on for so long. How must a scientist feel when, after years of experimenting, she finally proves her theory or discovers an important cure?

Whatever your dream may be, you can make it come true — but not instantly. As you saw on page 35, most dreams worth dreaming start with a step-by-step plan. And then it takes sticking to that plan. Will accomplishing your dream require practicing a skill every day? Will it take working with a teacher or coach regularly for some extra help?

Whatever you choose to do, it will take time, patience, and effort. And you will undoubtedly get frustrated at times. That's where the perseverance skill comes in. A person who keeps on practicing that foul shot when time after time the ball just misses the hoop is a person with — you guessed it! — perseverance. And that person is sure to achieve her goals!

Sticking-with-it situations

Your family got all excited about creating a web site about your summer vacation. Taking the pictures was the easy part. But it's fall already and those photos are still on memory cards. No web site yet! What if you said to yourself, "I'm going to spend 15 minutes a day creating the site" *and* you stuck with it until it was finished? With that kind of persistent effort, it really wouldn't take all that long. You'd finally have the vacation photos posted and Grandma would stop wondering where you all were in August!

Hmmm. What day was that?

> "If you want to get somewhere, you have to know where you want to go and how to get there. Then never, never, never give up."
> —Norman Vincent Peale, author

Think about how a "stick-to-it" attitude would make a difference here:

* You sign up for the indoor soccer league. You didn't realize that there are practices several nights a week and games every Saturday morning. Maybe you don't want to be on the team after all.
* Your classroom has hardly collected anything for the school canned-food drive. It's your job to remind your classmates every Monday morning how many weeks are left until the deadline. One kid keeps saying, "This is so lame. How could a can of tomato soup do anything?"

Now you try it!

See what happens when you …

* complete a family project that never seems to get finished: weeding the garden, cleaning out a closet, or organizing the music or movie collection.
* set a goal for physical activity, such as jumping rope 100 times without stopping, and work towards it daily.
* play your instrument for an additional 10 minutes every time you practice.
* work an extra five minutes a day on your homework or read two chapters in your book instead of one.

CRYSTAL POWER

Reaching goals takes perseverance, and slow, steady action over time. So does crystal formation. A diamond, for example, is a spectacular crystal that takes millions of years to form. Let these beautiful crystals inspire you to persevere as you watch them grow over several months.

What you need
- Water, 1 cup (250 ml)
- Small pot
- Packet of unflavored gelatin
- Spoon (for stirring)
- Sugar, 2½ cups (625 ml)
- Measuring cup
- Jar with lid
- Towel

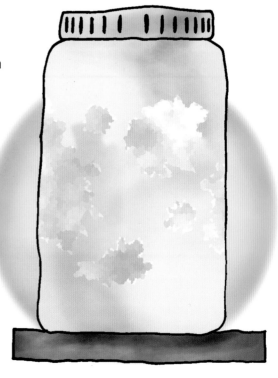

What you do

The crystal solution is very hot, so please ask an adult to help you prepare it.

1 Pour the water into the pot. Add the gelatin. On the stovetop, heat the mixture to just boiling, then turn off the heat. Stir to dissolve the gelatin.

2 Stir in the sugar, ½ cup (125 ml) at a time, until no more will dissolve.

3 Pour the clear liquid into the jar and secure the lid. Let any undissolved sugar remain at the bottom of the pot.

4 Wrap the jar in the towel to allow the liquid to cool very slowly (you'll get better crystals this way). Place the jar where it won't be disturbed and you can observe the crystals' growth. Remove the towel the next day.

5 It takes awhile for these crystals to appear, but it's well worth the wait! Check the jar each day, then each week, and even after a few months.

Creativity

IMAGINING AND MAKING SOMETHING NEW

You're watching the neighbor's kids while she goes to the market. They're bored with the same old toys. Quickly you invent a tossing game by wadding newspaper into balls and tossing them into a paper grocery bag. The kids love the game! You may not realize it, but you just showed the skill of *creativity* — the ability to imagine and create something new.

Yay!

People usually think about being creative through music, art, drama, or dance. Draw what's outside your window and you've captured your own unique view of the world. Play a tune on your clarinet. Even if it's a tune everyone knows, where you decide to play softly or loud, speed up or slow down the beat, or add a few notes makes it all your own. Invent new moves to a favorite song. These are all ways of using your imagination to create something new.

But the arts aren't the only way to be creative. Creativity is a mindset you can apply to any challenge. From designing a 50-story building that won't collapse in an earthquake to inventing a super sandwich from whatever happens to be in the refrigerator — that's creativity in action!

Creativity helps you come up with terrific new ideas to meet a challenge, solve problems, or imagine and produce something brand-new, even when the available materials are limited. What an awesome skill!

Taking the creative approach!

Your youth group is deciding on a fund-raising activity. You're really concerned about endangered animal habitats, and you're hoping that's the cause that gets chosen. The group leader has asked you to talk to the group about this issue, but bringing in a list of organizations the group could contribute money to doesn't seem like the most exciting way to get everyone on board. You want a more creative approach that will really get the others inspired to take on your cause.

To brainstorm ideas, check out the Creative-Thinking Jump Starts at right. How about a computer slide show? You love creating cards and invitations on the computer, but you've never put together a slide show. Then you remember your sister did one for her choral group — maybe she could help you out. You know you can get lots of great photos of animal habitats on the Internet.

Penguins are found at the South Pole, but not at the North Pole.

Your ideas start coming together and before you know it, you're imagining showing an awesome slide show at the next meeting. Your presentation uses the creativity skill by combining your interests and talents (computer graphics) and the available resources (your sister's skill and Internet photos) to produce something new and original.

How could a little creative thinking change these situations?

* Mom asks you to whip up something special for dessert. You can only use what's in the kitchen right now.
* You're camping with your Scout troop. One of your tentmates forgot her pillow.
* You're helping your family create this year's holiday mailing to friends and relatives. How can you make it more exciting than last year's letter?

Now you try it!

See what happens when you …

* think of another way to share information for a school project such as a brochure, skit, or original song lyrics.
* think of five uses for a paper clip, other than holding paper together.
* choreograph a dance routine or make up some new lyrics to your favorite song, instead of just sitting and listening to it.

CREATIVE-THINKING JUMP STARTS

When you want to spark your creative thinking, try following these steps. You don't have to follow them in this order or even use every step every time.

1. Investigate. Learn all you can about the challenge.

2. Innovate. Brainstorm several solutions or approaches.

3. Percolate. Give yourself time to think about each possibility. Why is one better than another?

4. Generate. Follow through on your best idea and give it a try.

5. Evaluate. How did it work? How could it be better?

Start creating! Grab a bag of drinking straws and a box of paper clips. How high of a tower can you create using only these two materials? Now see if you can create a structure that will support weight. Work with a friend, if you like. Or, have a competition with another team of friends and set a time limit.

Tip: You can open the paper clip like this to make a connector joint.

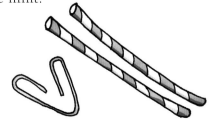

READY, SET, ACTION!

These motion games are a fun way to see how creative you can be. You'll need a few friends.

Kid Machine. Player A makes a simple, repetitive motion while standing in place. Player B makes different motions right next to Player A. Each new kid adds his body to the machine by adding a movement that fits with the others. Ask an unsuspecting adult to start up the machine by flipping the switch (kid A's arm). Let the action begin! For more fun, add weird sounds to the motions.

Sculpt-a-Kid. Make an amazing piece of art by "sculpting" your friends. Have one stand, squat, or curl up in an interesting shape. Add a few more players to your work by having them freeze their bodies in the shapes you create. Admire your creation!

PENNY FOR YOUR THOUGHTS

Use creative thinking to solve these penny problems!

* Arrange nine pennies into a triangle (one, three, and five pennies in each row). Change the triangle into a square by moving only two pennies.

* Using 10 pennies, make a triangle as shown. Moving only three pennies, make the triangle point in the opposite direction.

* Place three pennies in a row. Without touching the middle coin, can you rearrange the coins so the middle one is no longer in the center?

Resourcefulness

SEIZING OPPORTUNITIES

You've got your heart set on that new mountain bike that you saw at the store downtown, but even if you save every penny of your allowance, it would take a long time to own it. You know a lot of people in your neighborhood have dogs and you see them walking them every night after work. You're home most afternoons. *Hmmm*, how about starting a business as an after-school dog-walker? You could earn the money for that bike in no time. Now that's resourceful thinking!

> **Resourcefulness means ...** being able to act effectively or imaginatively and use initiative, especially when facing a challenge.

Some kids might say, "Boring, there's never anything to do around here." But when you have the character skill of *resourcefulness*, you're a kid who sees — and seizes — opportunities wherever you go. See your town library as a source for skateboarding know-how. See your school's kindergarten as a place to make a difference in younger kids' lives at lunchtime. See the Internet as a way to inspire your family to travel to a cool place over spring break. See a rainy day as a chance to organize your bedroom into a place all your own. And yes, see pet dogs as a way to earn money for something special!

There are so many exciting possibilities all around you (sometimes right before your eyes). Using those opportunities to get you closer to your goals is the sure sign of a resourceful person.

Resourcefulness to the rescue!

Tonight is the opening of the school play. The auditorium is filling up. It's 20 minutes to curtain time and no one can find the beautiful hats needed for scene 2. You are the prop manager. Instead of panicking, you ask a group of kids already seated if they would help you out by making hats from the craft paper left over from set design. You quickly show them how. While they do that, you spot the art teacher in the audience, and ask her if she has any feathers or netting you can use for the hats. She goes to get supplies from the art room. The kids really get into decorating the hats and they look great. You were able to figure out how to meet a challenge by putting cast-off materials, kids, and an art teacher together. And during intermission, you overhear so many folks talking about those "fabulous hats"!

How could a resourceful kid make the most of these other situations?

* Your friends are visiting and the power goes out. Uh-oh, now you need to entertain yourselves without using electricity.
* Your rock-climbing aunt is coming to visit. Rock climbing seems scary, but you're curious about the sport.
* You've always wanted to know how to macramé. You find out that your library has a collection of how-to books.

Now you try it!

See what happens when you …

* think of a way to turn a long, boring car trip into a good time for the whole family.
* ask a family member to share a talent with you.
* make a craft from recycled materials.

OPPORTUNITY CALENDAR

Make the most of the resources your community has to offer with this special calendar. Use it to keep track of upcoming events so you can plan ahead with family members. You'll have lots to look forward to!

What you need
- Sissors
- Glue stick
- Monthly calendar sheets (search under "calendar" on the Internet or photocopy a blank calendar)
- 12 sheets of construction paper, 12" x 18" (30 x 45 cm)
- Hole punch
- Ribbon or string
- Fine-point marker
- Round, color-coding, self-adhesive labels

What you do

1 Visit your local tourist information center and pick up brochures for museums, parks, and other interesting sites in your area. Gather local newspapers, events listings, and family magazines from markets or bookstores.

2 Organize a family meeting to look through the material and cut out announcements for places you'd like to visit and events you'd like to attend.

3 Glue a calendar page at the bottom of each piece of construction paper. Punch holes at the tops of the construction paper sheets and run ribbon or string through the holes to bind them together.

4 Use the marker to print the events on the labels. Decorate with mini-sketches or symbols. Then press the labels onto calendar date squares.

5 Use the top half of the sheet to paste announcements for events and sites you'd like to visit that month. Update your calendar monthly.

SEIZE-YOUR-CHANCE CARD GAME

Be resourceful and act quickly! Don't miss an opportunity to lay down your cards. The first player to get rid of all her cards wins.

What you need
- 2 to 4 players
- Deck of cards

What you do

1 Arrange cards as described: Set two piles of eight cards facedown in the center. Flip over the top cards and set them between the two piles. Deal the rest of the deck equally among the players, setting the dealt cards in facedown draw piles in front of each player.

2 Players shout, "Go!" to start the game. Each player makes a hand by drawing the top five cards from her pile. Cards can be set down from your hand if they are next in sequence — before or after either of the faceup cards in the center. If no one can go, players flip over the top cards from the side center piles until someone can make a move.

3 Players pick a new card from their draw pile so they always have five in their hand.

4 The first player to get rid of all cards from her hand and her pile is the winner!

TAKE CENTER STAGE!

What if you were watching a play — and saw an opportunity to join in? Have fun building your resourcefulness *and* your creative-thinking skills by stepping out of the audience right into the action on stage!

To start, you'll need a group of friends. Ask each one to gather several simple props. Two kids stand before the group and act out a scene. You can set the scene anywhere: walking to school, in the mall, hanging out in your room. Think of situations where you or the other actor would need to solve a problem, make the most of an opportunity, or use your imagination to respond to a challenge.

While the actors are performing, an audience member may shout, "Freeze" if she sees a chance to be involved in the drama. The actors must freeze, and the new player joins in. For example, she might be the clerk in the store where the first two actors were shopping. The play continues until everyone gets into the act.

*"*If opportunity doesn't knock, build a door."

—Milton Berle, actor and comedian

FREEZE!

You've seen how initiative, perseverance, focus, creativity, and resourcefulness are character skills that get kids doing awesome stuff. Now that you know what it takes to spend your time in exciting, productive ways, check out the list in RESOURCES on page 124 to see cool things you can learn or activities you can do. Have fun getting involved!

Doing the

Values and ideals are important concepts to think about and put into action when you are striving to become the best you can be. What do these words mean to you? *Values* are the big ideas that we value or hold important. Your values are a basic part of how you view the world and you use them every day (probably without even thinking about it some of time) as the basis for judging actions and events and for determining whether a way of behaving feels right or wrong. The word *ideal* means something that is perfect, and *ideals* are models of perfect ways to act. What do we mean by perfect actions? They are what's best for everyone, not just for ourselves. Of course, no one is perfect, and there's no way that every action you take could be perfect, but ideals give us standards to try to live by.

Your actions say a lot about your values and ideals, which in turn reflect the kind of person you are. So, think about how *you* make choices. Do you do what's fun and easy for you or just go along with what all the other kids are doing? Or, do you stop and think about what you believe is best for everyone or what your gut instincts tell you is really right (what is fair or honest, for example), and then decide what to do?

Values and ideals can guide everyday decisions. For example, do you appreciate a clean environment? Do you think you have a responsibility to care for the Earth? If so, then even something as ordinary as drinking a can of soda is a chance to demonstrate these important beliefs. Now you must decide what to do with the can. The easiest thing to do would be to just drop it on the ground. Of course your neighborhood would look like a garbage dump in no time if

Right Thing!

USING VALUES AND IDEALS TO GUIDE YOUR ACTIONS

everyone made that choice. You could throw the can in the trash. Or, you could take the time to recycle the can. That last choice takes a bit more effort, but it is a choice that is best for everyone (wildlife, too!). You just helped save the Earth's precious resources. One person — you! — can make small choices that make a big difference.

What character skills does it take to be a kid who acts thoughtfully and carefully in ways that reflect his or her important beliefs?

Responsibility. People can depend on you. You stand behind your actions.

Fairness. You understand that all people must be treated fairly. The same standards and rules apply to everyone.

Appreciation. You are thankful for what makes the world an awesome place. What's more, you want to do your share to make others value that also. You appreciate what others do for you — and you take the time to let them know!

Optimism. Your hopeful outlook propels you to take action to improve a situation. And when you take action, it's more likely things really will turn out positively.

Integrity. You act in sync with your values. You care about what's right and follow through to make the right choices.

Are you ready to let your values and ideals guide your actions? You'll find that when you do good in the world, you'll be doing yourself a world of good, too!

Responsibility
"OWNING" YOUR ACTIONS

Are you a responsible kid people can depend on? Thinking about the way you typically act at home, at school, and with friends, answer these questions and see.

Do you *take care of what needs to be done?*
When something needs to be done, do you ignore it or do you follow through and get it finished?
If there is something you are supposed to do, do you wait for an adult to remind you, or do you do it on your own?

Are you *accountable (do you own up to your actions)?*
If things go wrong, do you make excuses and blame others or do you answer for your actions?

Are you *trustworthy?*
If people trust you with something, whether it's one of their possessions like a CD player or personal information that they ask you to keep confidential, do you pay no attention and act carelessly or are you reliable?
If you make a promise, do you break it or keep it?

Do you *have good judgment?*
When you make a decision, do you think about which choice is the easiest one, or which choice is right for everyone involved?

You can probably tell that the second choice in each question is the responsible answer every time. It's easy to see on a short quiz what's the right thing to do. What's not so easy is to always be responsible in real life. Taking responsibility can sometimes seem like a burden. And your friends may choose different actions, which can make it hard to stick to your decision. But when you consider others, you benefit, too.

The more responsible you are, the more responsibility you'll be trusted with. For example, if you always get your homework finished on time, your mom is more likely to let you spend the night at your friend's house even if you have lots of homework that weekend. Or, if you always return your friend's CDs in good condition, he's more likely to loan you a video game. You will discover that taking on *responsibility* gives you personal power. The more others can depend on you, the more you can depend on yourself and take charge of your life!

Being responsible means ...

- following through on things; being dependable and reliable.
- making your own choices between right and wrong.
- being able to take charge of or be trusted with important matters.

Making the responsible choice

You've agreed to take care of your neighbors' cats this weekend while they're away. Then you find out your cousin is coming to town with her parents and wants you to hang out with her. She's even invited you to spend the night in her motel with her. You hardly ever get to see these relatives and they have a whole weekend of fun adventures planned. But you made a commitment to the neighbors, and Powderpuff and Skit are depending on you! What are you going to do? Wait, your friend from Scouts loves cats and volunteers at the humane society. How about explaining all the procedures to her? You can check with your neighbors to be sure it's OK with them. Before you head off for the day, you can check on the cats and feed them in the morning. Then you can stay in touch with your friend in case she has any problems. Rather than calling the neighbors to cancel the arrangement you agreed to, you followed through on your commitment, showing that you're dependable.

How might a responsible kid act in these other situations?

* Your friend loans you his video game station. You accidentally drop it. It looks OK.
* You tell your coach you'll be at the game, but later in the day you're more in the mood to watch TV.
* You notice that all the paper used at your school is thrown in the dumpster and not recycled.

Sorry, dude. This was totally my fault.

Now you try it!

See what happens when you …

* take care of something someone trusts you with and return it promptly.
* cheerfully agree to do a chore when asked and then promptly follow through on completing it.
* take the blame and apologize if something is your fault.

RESPONSIBILITY IN ACTION!

Set some goals for actions that you feel responsible about. Then decorate this book to remind and inspire you!

What you need
- 4 half-sheets of colored paper, 4¼" x 11" (10.5 x 27.5 cm)
- Stapler
- Markers
- Scissors
- Old magazines
- Glue
- Colored pencils

What you do

1 Arrange and fold the sheets of paper as shown.

2 Open the fold and staple on it to hold the sheets together. Refold to form a tall booklet with pages that stick out like tabs. On the top cover, write *I am responsible* .... Label the tabs as shown, then decorate the pages with drawings and cutouts.

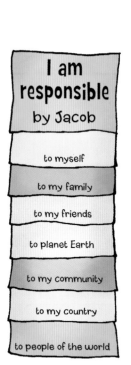

I am responsible
by Jacob
to myself
to my family
to my friends
to planet Earth
to my community
to my country
to people of the world

CLICK!
to planet Earth
to my community
to my country
to people of the world

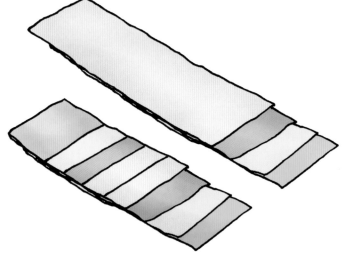

AN "EGG-STRAORDINARY" RESPONSIBILITY

Take care of this hard-boiled "critter" for a day. Can you keep it safe?

What you need

- Hard-boiled egg
- Markers
- Glue
- Yarn
- Glitter
- Sequins
- Small basket or box
- Tissue paper, shredded paper, or bubble wrap

What you do

1 So, you're the proud caretaker of this newborn baby critter. OK, so it looks just like a hard-boiled egg. Well then, your first job is to decorate it. Give it a face. Glue on yarn hair, glitter, sequins, whatever you like. It's your critter!

2 Think of a name for your baby critter. Is it a boy or a girl?

3 Use the basket or box as a carrier. Decorate it with your critter's name. Put in the soft materials to keep your critter from getting broken.

4 Be responsible for your critter for at least a day. Take it everywhere you go: in the car, to your friend's house, or out on the playground. You must be very careful with your critter. It's very fragile and will break easily. Your critter can rest in the refrigerator overnight. How many days can you keep your critter safe?

Think about it!

What was it like to be responsible for something?
What part was the hardest?
What was most fun?
Do you think you were a good caretaker?

This is egg-citing!

"**D**on't spend your precious time asking, 'Why isn't the world a better place?' It will only be time wasted. The question to ask is, 'How can I make it better?' To that there is an answer."

—Leo F. Buscaglia, author

Ryan Hreljac: taking responsibility for clean water

On a trip to South Africa in 2003, Ryan Hreljac saw firsthand how some Africans who don't have access to wells get their water.

"The world is like a great big puzzle and we all have to figure out where our puzzle piece fits. I figure my piece fits with clean water. I just hope everyone else finds out where their puzzle piece fits, too."

—Ryan Hreljac

Do you feel responsible for making sure all children get clean water to drink? Ryan Hreljac from Ontario, Canada, does. When he was 6 years old, he learned at school that kids in Africa were dying because they didn't have clean water. "I didn't feel right about that," he says. "I got really, really upset."

That feeling got Ryan started on a goal. He set out to earn the $70 he thought would be enough to drill a well in Africa. After four months of doing extra chores around the house, he brought his earnings to WaterCan, an organization that provides clean water to poor countries. There he was told it actually costs $2,000 to drill a well. Ryan wasn't discouraged, however. He just got busy doing more chores. News of Ryan's project spread and soon Ryan had received enough donations to meet his new goal. In 2000, Ryan traveled with his parents to the Angolo Primary School in Uganda to see his well. He met the children who enjoy clean water because of his dream and hard work.

Since that first well, Ryan has traveled all over the world raising money for clean water. With the support of other organizations, Ryan's Well Foundation has built more than 200 wells in Africa, South America, and Asia. The World of Children and UNICEF awarded Ryan the Founder's Award for his amazing work. Ryan plans to become a water engineer when he grows up. "I want everyone in the world to have clean water," he says.

Fairness

DOING RIGHT BY OTHERS

Play fair. Take turns. Share. You've heard these words ever since you were a little kid. They remind us to treat others as we would like to be treated — fairly. Fair treatment, or justice, is something everyone understands and wants to live by.

Sometimes life seems just outright unfair — such as when a kid does great on a test without studying or a family loses its home in a hurricane. But the rules we agree to live by and our daily actions can be held to a standard of fairness. Imagine how kids would feel if the umpire allowed five strikes before a player was out on one team but the other team only got three. What if your teacher allowed only the brown-eyed students to have 15 extra minutes at lunchtime? What if the cafeteria gave free choice of drinks only to the girls?

Fairness means ...

- not favoring any one person more than another.
- following what is just, especially in the way you treat people or make decisions.

Strike five!

How can you be sure your actions demonstrate the character skill of *fairness*? Use the Golden Rule — *Treat others as you want to be treated* — as your ideal. If you act in a way that you wouldn't want to be treated if you were in that same situation, you break the rule. Follow the Golden Rule and you'll put the spirit of fairness into action and uphold the important value of justice.

Practicing fair play

When you're playing soccer, a few kids always hog the ball. In fact, there's one kid in particular who never gets to be part of the play because no one passes to her. "Ashley's not a very good player," those ball-hoggers say. "It's all about winning, you know." You think about how this attitude is so unfair to Ashley. You also remember what the coach said, "It's not about winning. It's about how you play the game and about everyone having a good time." You decide to talk to your coach and other players. "Let's give everyone a chance. It's only fair! And you know what? Each of us will become a stronger player when we all get a chance to play!"

How might you put the spirit of fairness into action in these other situations?

* Your good friend tells you she didn't have time to study for a test. She wants you to let her copy your test.
* Your friend comes to your house. You tell him you'll decide what you'll do together because it's your house. He tells you he doesn't think that's fair.
* There's one piece of cake left from last night. You and your brother both love cake. "It's mine," you think. "I'm older."

Now you try it!

See what happens when you …

* figure out a fair way for you and your friends to decide which movie to rent at the video store.
* give up your turn to someone who never seems to get a chance.
* let a younger brother or sister make a choice you usually make.

PLAY PIGS – FAIRLY AND <u>UN</u>FAIRLY

When you play a game, each player has to follow the same rules. Ever thought about why that is? Play a few rounds of Pigs, a classic dice game. Then try changing the rules to make it unfair for one or two of the players and see what happens. Let everyone have a chance to experience how the unfair rules make them feel. Does everyone still enjoy the game? Be sure to finish with a few fair rounds so everyone has a good time!

> "**J**ustice cannot be for one side alone, but must be for both."
>
> —Eleanor Roosevelt, former First Lady and United Nations diplomat

What you need

- Die
- Paper
- Pencil

Let's play

To take a turn, a player rolls the die. Any number rolled other than 1 starts the player's total for that turn. After each roll, the player can either roll again, or *hold* (stop rolling). If the player holds, the sum of the rolls during that turn is added to his score, and it becomes the next player's turn. But here's the catch. If the player rolls a 1 (the "oinker"), he scores nothing for that entire turn and it becomes the next player's turn. When a player reaches a total of 100 points or more, he wins and the game ends.

Try an unfair rule: For one of the players, an "oinker" is 1 *and* 2.

OINKER!

A worldwide charter

Did you know that every person in the world is entitled to fair treatment? A *charter* is a formal written document that spells out certain rights and privileges. The Charter of the United Nations sets forth important guiding ideals and values to make the world a better place. Here, in the words of the charter, are just a few of the principles it outlines:

> *We the Peoples of the United Nations Determined …*
> *to reaffirm faith in fundamental human rights, in the dignity and worth of the human person, in the equal rights of men and women and of nations large and small …*

WRITE YOUR OWN CHARTER

Try this activity with a group of friends. On a piece of "parchment paper," write a statement of fairness and equal treatment for all. Here are some ideas you might declare:

> *We should treat others as we would like to be treated.*
> *We must take responsibility to see that everyone is treated fairly.*
> *We must take care of the Earth so that all life is treated fairly.*

We must take care of the Earth so that all life is treated fairly.

What you need
- Sheet of white paper
- Cookie sheet
- Cold coffee or tea, ½ cup (125 ml)
- Markers or pens
- Yarn

Here are some ways to put your charter into action!

Set a Fairness Goal. Every week, see if you can perform at least one act of fairness or of putting the Golden Rule into action.

Keep a Justice Journal. Do you see unfair acts around you? Note them in your Journal. Then write ideas for what you can do to make something unfair, fair.

Gather Friends for Fairness. Many voices are stronger than one, so join with other kids to do these activities.

What you do

1 Rip the edges of the paper. Crumple it into a ball, then flatten it.

2 Place the paper on the cookie sheet. Pour coffee or tea over it. Swoosh it around to completely cover the paper. Let it sit for about five minutes. Then pour off the liquid. Let the paper dry.

3 Write your message. Add a drawing of the fair world you envision. Roll up your document like a scroll and tie it with yarn. Or, display as an inspirational reminder to everyone to act in the spirit of fairness and justice.

> **"Fairness** is what justice really is."
>
> —Potter Stewart, former U.S. Supreme Court associate justice

MAKE A GOLDEN RULER

Think what a wonderful world it would be if everyone practiced the Golden Rule. Make a Golden Ruler to remind everyone to measure his or her actions by the important standard of fairness.

What you need

- Scissors
- Gold foil paper
- Glue
- Cardboard strip, 1" x 6" (2.5 x 15 cm)
- Thin permanent marker
- Ruler
- Hole punch
- Yarn

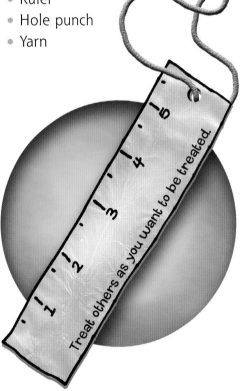

What you do

1 Cut two strips of gold foil and glue one on each side of the cardboard strip.

2 Across the top of one side, mark ½" (1 cm) and 1" (2.5 cm) points. Add small numbers to create a 6" (15 cm) ruler.

3 Write this message across the bottom: *Treat others as you want to be treated.*

4 Punch a hole near one end and tie a length of yarn through it. Hang the ruler anywhere in your home. You can even wear it as a necklace!

Appreciation

VALUING WHAT'S IMPORTANT

Appreciation means ...

- having feelings of being thankful or grateful.
- enjoying and valuing what's good about your life or what's important to you.

Twinkling stars in the night sky … extra-creamy chocolate pudding … a kitten picking your lap as a spot to cuddle … a special friend who always listens when you're upset … an adult who takes extra time to help you solve a problem ….

Taking time to acknowledge and feel thankful for things like these, small and large, means you appreciate them. And when you feel grateful, you can't help but be inspired to say "thank you" to those who make the world an awesome place. What's more, you'll want to do your share to make others feel this gratitude, too. So, are you eager to make *appreciation* and gratitude a part of your outlook on life? Here's how!

Know what's good. What brings you joy? What makes our lives better? What makes the world a better place? From your favorite ice cream to our families to a country where we can live in freedom … these are all good things that we appreciate.

Look for it. Take time to see the good that's all around you. Does your little brother or your dog always welcome you home? Has the rainy day helped you discover a favorite game you forgot about? Do you love looking at your neighbor's garden on your way to school? Don't take anything for granted. Think about the joy you receive throughout the day, and you'll feel grateful.

Just say thanks. You know how you feel when someone thanks you for your help or for something nice you did. Everyone appreciates a thank-you. So when people do good things, say "thank you so much!" to let them know you notice and care. You'll show you appreciate how they take time to make the world a better place.

Create more! What good can you do to make others feel thankful? A smile, a kind word, an act of kindness are all ways to spread joy. You'll be creating feelings of appreciation and gratitude at the same time!

Have an attitude of gratitude

Freeze! Can you think of five things to be grateful for? Start brainstorming: Someone just gave you this book. Hey, you know how to read! The couch you are sitting on is comfy. You little brother isn't bugging you at the moment. Whatever's cooking for dinner smells pretty good … Wow, didn't that feel good? Life is OK after all. Now go one step further and thank someone responsible for making your life better. "Hey, Mom! Dinner smells great. Thanks for making roast chicken!" You probably just made your mom grateful for having you in her life!

Practice having an attitude of gratitude, anytime, anywhere. Brainstorm at least five things to be grateful for in these situations. Then think of ways to say thank you for at least one of them.

* Your family is stuck in traffic, just when you're trying to go on vacation.
* Your Scout troop is camped by a beautiful lake where the swimming is awesome, but there sure are a lot of mosquitoes.
* You didn't get to practice your violin very much last week and today is your lesson.

> "**N**ever take anything for granted."
> —Benjamin Disraeli, former prime minister of Britain

Thank You
(ENGLISH)

Merci
(FRENCH mare-SEE)

Gracias
(SPANISH GRAH-see-ess)

Danke
(GERMAN DAHN-kuh)

Now you try it!

See what happens when you …

* say thank you to someone you have never thanked before.
* think of something positive about someone you dislike.
* think back on three things you appreciated at the end of the day.

GRATITUDE JOURNAL

Create a journal that says, "Thank You!" Make it all your own. Decorate the cover with pictures of things you appreciate. You might use drawings, personal photos, or words and pictures from magazines. Fill a page each day with words and sketches to express your gratitude.

What you need

- Sheet of construction paper for the cover
- White paper (as many sheets as you like for the pages)
- Hole punch
- Yarn, 3' (1 m)
- Markers
- Scissors
- Old magazines
- Glue

What you do

1 Fold the construction paper in half. Fold the stack of white paper in half and place it inside the cover.

2 Punch holes about ½" (1 cm) apart along the spine. Weave the yarn up, then back down through the holes as shown. Tie the yarn in a bow at the bottom.

3 Decorate the cover with drawings or cutout pictures. Make gratitude entries as often as you like. Here are some ideas: what I am thankful for, what brightened my day, my gifts of kindness to others.

Optimism

MAINTAINING A POSITIVE VIEW

Let's face it, the world is a complicated place. Wonderful things happen every day. The sun rises. Babies are born. People can be so kind to each other. But horrible things happen, too. There are tsunamis, hurricanes, and earthquakes. Pollution destroys wildlife. People fight wars and are sometimes so cruel to each other. It would be easy to feel discouraged … or to feel hopeful that things can improve. Which attitude reflects how *you* see the world?

Optimism is a positive view of the future and of life in general. When you are optimistic, you believe things will turn out well. With this hopeful outlook, you are more willing to take action to improve a situation. And when you take action, it is more likely things really will turn out positively in the end!

Pessimism is just the opposite. With a negative outlook, you believe things won't get better, so why even bother to try? With that attitude, it's more likely things will stay as they are or maybe even get worse. People say that optimism and pessimism are "self-fulfilling prophesies." That means that what you think will happen, does happen. Your decision to act or not is determined by your outlook.

It's not that optimists don't see the real problems of the world or that they never get discouraged. But they see beyond the problems and the minor setbacks to the solutions (see Ryan Hreljac, page 58). Optimists think, *I can do something to make this situation better.* Their actions create the positive change they hope for. That's why optimism is such a powerful character skill to possess!

> ## Optimism means ...
> - having a positive, hopeful, or cheerful attitude or view of the world.
> - believe or expecting that things will turn out well.

I know I can do this!

The power of optimism

It's your first time at summer camp. You don't know any of the other kids, and you're having some trouble making friends. The pessimist might think, *No one seems to likes me, so what's the point in even trying.* The optimist would think, *It takes time to get to know people. Maybe these other kids are feeling shy, too. I need to be a friend to make a friend, so I'll take the first step.* Can you see how an optimistic attitude leads to taking action in a way that changes a situation for the better?

Practice some positive thinking! How might an optimist react in these situations?

* You don't make it onto the swim team.
* You forget your homework.
* You smash up your bike, but you are OK.

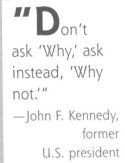

"**D**on't ask 'Why,' ask instead, 'Why not.'"
—John F. Kennedy, former U.S. president

Now you try it!

See what happens when you …

* tell other kids in your group that the project is going to turn out well, then lead them in coming up with ideas to be sure it does.
* have a great day? No! *Do* something to *make* it a great day.
* try again if you don't succeed at first.

RAINBOWS: SYMBOLS OF OPTIMISM

Catching sight of a rainbow lifts everyone's spirits. Rainbows are the symbol of hope and optimism. Why? They mean the end of stormy weather! Pounding rain, threatening clouds, howling winds … and suddenly the sun brightens the sky and a rainbow appears! You can create your own rainbows to remind everyone of the power of optimism!

> "In the middle of difficulty lies opportunity."
> —Albert Einstein, scientist

Rainbow Reflection

What you need
- Shallow pan about ¾ full of water
- Mirror
- Rock
- Strong light source such as a lamp, flashlight, or direct sunlight coming through a window
- White paper

What you do

1 Set up the pan, mirror, rock, and light source as shown.

2 Position the white paper so the reflected light shines onto it. Adjust the mirror until you can see the watery reflection of a rainbow on the paper!

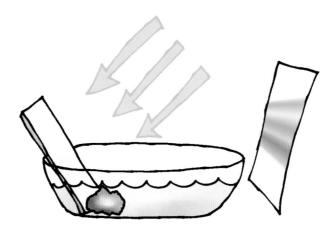

CD Rainbows
Hold a CD near a white wall. Shine a flashlight on the CD. Tip the CD and move the flashlight so that a rainbow is reflected on the wall. Keep moving the CD and flashlight. What happens to the colors?

Water-Spray Rainbows

On a very sunny day, turn on the garden hose and hold your thumb over the blast to create a veil of tiny droplets. Standing with your back to the sunlight, move around until you see a rainbow in the spray.

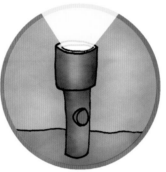

Rainbows in the Dark

In a dark room, stand a flashlight on end. Look at it through a nylon stocking. Now view the light through a feather or gauzy scarf. Notice the rainbow patterns.

Slick Rainbows

Fill a glass with water. Let a drop of clear nail polish fall onto the water's surface. Move your head until you see a swirling rainbow of color in the polish.

Rain-Blows

Blow bubbles in the sunlight. Look closely at the skin of the soapy spheres. You'll see swirling rainbows!

Why do we see rainbows?

When light travels in a straight line, we see it as white or clear light. But visible light is really a mix of colors called a *spectrum*. When light's straight path is bent in just the right way, the light separates into that spectrum, which we call a rainbow. Water, water droplets, the tiny metal ridges of a CD, even your eyelashes are all substances that can bend and separate a beam of light into the spectrum. A rainbow's colors always appear in the same order: **r**ed, **o**range, **y**ellow, **g**reen, **b**lue, **i**ndigo, and **v**iolet. You can remember the order by thinking of the man's name, ROY G. BIV.

Integrity
BEING TRUE TO YOUR VALUES

Integrity comes from a Latin word you may have heard in math class, *integer*, meaning a whole number. What does integrity have to do with something whole? A person with *integrity* is whole, complete, undivided, and consistent through and through. She knows what she values and acts in ways that are true to certain ideals. Her beliefs and actions are the same. A person with integrity "does the right thing," even when that is a difficult choice.

Some decisions don't take integrity. It really doesn't matter whether you order an ice-cream cone or a milkshake. But other decisions are important. How you choose your friends, for example. Or, how you spend your time. Whenever you stop and think about whether something is right or wrong, you are taking the first step in acting with integrity. You are using your values and ideals to guide your choice. It's not always easy to make these big decisions. Thinking through the answers to the questions below will help you make choices that show you to be a person with the character skill of integrity.

Integrity Checklist
* What are my ideals? What do I value? What is important to me?
* How will this choice or action reflect my beliefs?
* How would I want to be treated in the same situation?
* How will I feel later, after I make my decision?
* Might I hurt anyone (even myself)?
* Might I help anyone (even myself)?
* What would a person I respect think of my decision?

Integrity means ...
- acting in a way that's honest and sincere.
- having ideals and values and using them to guide you in your actions.

When you know what is right, when you care about what is right, and when you do what you believe is right, you are acting with integrity.

Integrity in action!

A group of kids is picking on a kid you don't really like. They want you to join in. Something in your gut tells you it just isn't right. "Go ahead," they say. "He won't do anything about it. It doesn't matter." Here's where integrity comes in. It does matter to you. In fact, it matters enough that you find the courage to tell your friends, "I don't like Jason any better than you guys, but I'm not going to stoop to picking on him. It makes me feel like a creep for acting that way. No one deserves to be picked on. I'm walking away. Come on, let's do something cool. Making fun of Jason isn't."

How can integrity help you make the right choice in these situations?

Boy, she gave me **way** too much change.

* Your friend's parents give him permission to be at your house. He goes to the movies instead. He asks you to lie about his whereabouts if they call.
* You are alone in your classroom. You are standing near the teacher's reward box. It would be so easy to grab that cute reward trinket you've been wanting.
* You buy a burger. The cashier is distracted and accidentally gives you too much change.

"**E**very time you stand up for an ideal, you send forth a tiny ripple of hope."
—Robert Kennedy, former U.S. attorney general

Now you try it!

Discuss with your friends and family who shows (or doesn't show) integrity …
* during a favorite television show.
* in a news story you hear about.
* during an actual event from your lives.

Compare ideas of how those involved could change their actions to act with integrity.

Craig Kielburger:
inspired by his ideals to help the world's children

At age 14, Craig Kielburger traveled to Brazil to learn more about child laborers in that country. After a game of soccer with a group of street children, he received what he describes as "the most important material gift of his life," a Brazilian soccer jersey from Jose, a young street child. It remains framed on his wall to this day.

When Craig Kielburger was 12 years old, he read an article in a Toronto newspaper that shocked him deeply. It was a story about the murder of Iqbal Masih. Iqbal was a Pakistani boy the same age as Craig who had been a slave in a carpet factory. Iqbal had never been to school. Instead, he had worked 16 hours a day in the factory since he was four years old. After Iqbal ran away, he made it his mission to let the world know about the horrors of child slavery. He gave speeches around the world about his life as a slave. He won awards and appeared on television. When Iqbal was 12 years old, he was murdered, a crime that remains unsolved.

Now who would tell the world about the injustice of child slavery? Craig began to learn more about the terrible truth that every year, thousands of children in poor countries are kidnapped and forced to work in factories. They work long hours in cruel and dangerous conditions. Craig knew it would be difficult to change this situation, but he also knew he had to try. With the help of five friends from school, Craig founded Free The Children and began advocating for these victims of child slavery. FTC has since grown into the largest international network of children helping children affected by issues of child labor, poverty, and war.

Young people do have "a positive role to play through very simple, very concrete actions," Craig says. "Maybe it's a petition, or a letter-writing campaign, or a small fund-raiser like a bake sale or a car wash. But it empowers them to realize they can make a difference on some level. And it teaches them that even small actions can help change the world."

> "I won't give up until the exploitation of all children has ended and all children have their rights."
> —Craig Kielburger

TEST YOUR INTEGRITY

In order to win this game, you'll need to make decisions that reflect integrity — and your friends will be the judges!

What you need
- White paper
- Glue
- Stiff cardboard
- Different-colored flat beads or buttons or small photos of the players and milk-jug caps
- Pens or pencils
- Index cards
- Die

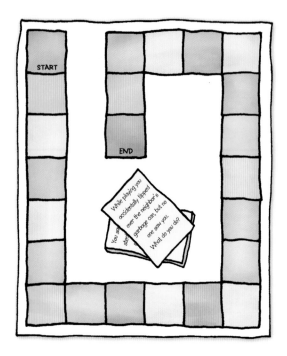

How to set up

1 Create this game board (or search online under "game board templates"). Glue the game board onto cardboard.

2 For markers, use the beads or buttons. Or, glue a small photo of each player onto milk-jug caps.

3 Make a set of about 20 integrity cards by writing a *dilemma* (a situation where you are faced with a difficult choice) on each index card. You can copy questions and situations from this book, or make up your own. Have players each add dilemmas of their own before starting the game.

Let's play!

1 A player rolls the die, takes a card, and answers the question. The group decides if the player has answered with integrity. If so, the player moves the number of dots on the die.

2 The first player to reach the end of the game wins. Continue playing to find out who comes in second, third, and fourth place.

"The time is always right to do what is right."
—Martin Luther King, Jr., civil rights activist

TAKE-A-STAND WRISTBAND

What do you believe in, value, or think is important? *Caring? Fairness? Creativity?* Let the world know by wearing wristbands displaying these powerful ideas. Pick your own word or one from the table of contents at the beginning of this book.

What you need

- Clean, empty plastic milk jug
- Scissors
- Ruler
- Hole punch
- Fine-point permanent marker
- Yarn

What you do

1 From milk-jug plastic, cut wristband strips to fit around your wrist (about ¾" x 5½"/2 x 13.5 cm). You may need adult help here.

2 Round the corners of the strips. Use the hole punch to make holes at the ends.

3 On each strip, use the marker to write a word for a value, ideal, or idea you feel strongly about. Use cool lettering like all capitals, bold, cursive, or italics.

4 Loop yarn though the holes. Place the bracelet on your wrist. Have a friend help you secure it with a bow. Wear with pride!

• •

Think about what you value. What can you take *responsibility* for? How can you make things *fairer* for everyone? What do you *appreciate* and how can you give others something to feel grateful for? What do you feel *optimistic* you can change? Do you have the *integrity* to stay true to what you value? See RESOURCES on page 124 for ways to match your values and your interests with actions. Let your values lead you to doing the right thing! You'll be making a difference … in the world and in yourself.

Going After

Can you go through the day without finding at least one fascinating thing you want to learn more about? Probably not! That's your natural curiosity at work, inspiring you to explore our amazing world. Going after knowledge — getting smarter about all kinds of things and filling your mind with exciting ideas — is the way we discover new things about what's all around us. Learning is finding out what's true, whether it's what Mars is made of, what microscopic bacteria eat, or how people survive in desert climates. It's also the key to knowing how to do lots of things that are cool and fun, like setting up a web page, knitting yourself a scarf, or making ice cream. Wow! Going after knowledge is very powerful.

Pretend your brain is a muscle. Using it regularly, even stretching it a bit to understand a difficult idea or to try a skill that is a little challenging, is the best way to keep it in top shape! And learning new things is a super way to do just that. Having an active mind also makes you a more interesting person, with facts and opinions to share. Think about the people you like to spend time with — what makes them fun to be around? Do they always have interesting things to tell you and do you often come away with something new to think about? What's more, when you have knowledge, you have something powerful to contribute to make the world better in some way.

People who strive to be their best value learning because they understand that it helps them achieve their goals. Learning is very important to them and they look for opportunities to learn new things whenever they can. Chances are you also understand how important it is to keep learning new things,

Knowledge!

DEVELOPING A PASSION FOR LEARNING ABOUT THE WORLD

but you might not have thought about it in quite this way before. Going after knowledge doesn't only happen at school. Maybe you're a straight A student, and maybe you aren't — but you are still a learner. After all, you find the world a pretty cool place and you like to think, explore, and discover, right? Let's see what skills you need to do more of that!

Curiosity. It all starts with an "I wonder" or an "I want to know" attitude.

Discovery. You are eager to learn all you can and you know how to find out more about what interests you.

Sharing what you know. You find it exciting to exchange the knowledge and new ideas you gain with others. Your knowledge has the power to make the world a better place.

Enthusiasm. You see learning as a fun and exciting part of every day. You've realized that the more you know about the world, the more interesting a place it is to live in.

Learning on your own. You take charge of your own learning. When you don't know something, you dig in and find the answer!

When you develop a passion for learning about the world, you take a huge step toward becoming the best you can be! You have fun, too, because you're always making discoveries about awesome stuff that interests you as well as about things you never realized could be so fascinating. The going after knowledge trait is one you'll use just about anytime, anyplace, for the rest of your life, so let's try out the skills you'll need to develop it.

Curiosity

PURSUING YOUR SENSE OF WONDER

Curiosity means ...

- having a strong desire to learn something new.
- wondering why certain things are so.

Curiosity is the first step toward learning something new. You start to wonder, and *hmmm* … before you know it, your curiosity has you hooked. It gets you discovering more about everything — from knowing about yourself and the world close to you, to knowing about times long ago and far-off galaxies.

So what do *you* want to know? What more could you learn about your favorite animal? What do you want to know about an author or athlete you really admire? How does a photo or an e-mail message travel over the Internet? What will a car look like 20 years from now? Develop the *curiosity* skill by pondering the why, where, what, when, how, and if about the things that interest you. Ask questions and be eager to find the answers.

See where a sense of wonder takes you!

You're bike-riding with a friend, and every time you squeeze your brakes, they stop the bike but not without making a really loud screechy noise. Your friend says you need to stop in at the bike shop and have your front wheel "trued." Wow! How'd she know that? You watch the mechanic carefully adjust your wheel. This looks cool! You wonder how you could do some of your own repairs. Your curiosity sends you home with a working bike *and* a manual on bike tune-ups!

Where would a curious mind lead you in these other situations?

* Your mom tells you that your grandpa came to America from China 50 years ago. You wonder what his life was like when he was a kid.
* You're taking a hike with your family. Your younger brother sees a long, narrow bird's nest dangling from a branch and asks you what kind of bird made it, but you don't know.
* Your homework is to write a reptile report. Sounds pretty dull, you think. Then you search the Internet for reptiles and you come up with the most amazing creatures: skinks, legless lizards, goannas, and warrajans! *Hmmm …* this is going to be pretty interesting after all.

There are no **Penguins** at the North Pole, only the South Pole.

The **Basilisk lizard** can run on water.

Now you try it!

See what happens when you find out …

* *why* something happens, like why the moon seems to change shape.
* *how* to do something, like skateboard or knit.
* *how* a common item is made, such as how a CD is produced.
* *why* a favorite creature behaves a particular way, like why frogs croak.

> "The cure for boredom is curiosity. There is no cure for curiosity."
>
> —Ellen Parr, author

WONDER, THEN DISCOVER WHY!

You might think science is all about complicated formulas, technical equipment, and textbooks. But most scientists will tell you it's *really* all about being curious. That's because scientists try to understand and explain the world. How do they figure out what's going on? The first step is to observe and wonder. The next step is to experiment and discover why.

Magic Milk Pond

Ever wondered how pond insects walk on water?

What you need

- Milk
- Plate
- Food colorings
- Toothpick
- Liquid detergent

What you do

1 Pour enough milk on the plate to completely cover the bottom.

2 When the milk is still, drip different food colorings on it.

3 Dip a toothpick in the detergent. Place it in the middle of the color drops.

4 What do you observe? What do you wonder?

What did you discover?

The drops of food coloring explode and swirl. Why? The milk is made up of liquid *molecules* (the smallest particle a substance can be divided into and still be that substance). They cling to and tug on each other, connecting and stretching the surface of the liquid so it's like a skin. This force is called *surface tension*. The coloring floats on top of that skin. Adding soap weakens the surface tension. Now the milk molecules move around, swirling the food coloring drops into colorful explosions.

Surface tension on a pond is strong enough to support small, very lightweight insects such as water striders. Their legs barely dent the water's surface, allowing them to walk on water!

"Dancing" Rice

Are you curious about how we hear sound?

What you need

- Plastic wrap
- Bowl
- Handful of raw rice
- Cookie sheet
- Spoon

What you do

1 Stretch plastic wrap tightly over the bowl.

2 Scatter the rice over the wrap.

3 Hold the cookie sheet near the bowl and whack the sheet with the spoon.

4 What do you observe? What do you wonder?

What did you discover?

The loud noise causes the rice to "dance." Why? The air near the crash *vibrates* (moves back and forth very quickly). Airwaves travel in all directions. The waves hit the plastic wrap, making it vibrate and causing the rice to move. The airwaves also hit your eardrums, making them vibrate, and you hear the crash.

"**M**ere curiosity adds wings to every step."
—Johann Wolfgang von Goethe, author

Discovery

FILLING YOUR BRAIN WITH AWESOME INFORMATION!

Discovery means ...
finding out about something new or learning something that you didn't know.

Knowledge is information and ideas. It's knowing the chances of your softball game getting rained out as well as knowing what causes the rain. It's knowing how to bake the best chocolate chip cookies ever as well as knowing who were the first people to eat chocolate. All knowledge is powerful because it helps you take action: setting goals, making smart decisions, taking a different approach when something isn't working, or learning a skill you can enjoy and take pride in.

Being a knowledge go-getter means you're skilled at *discovery*. You know where to find all kinds of information and ideas. Your classroom, the library, the Internet, and museums are all rich sources. So are the lake, a park, and your own backyard. People are amazing sources of knowledge, too. Everyone is an expert about something, and people are usually happy to share what they know.

> So you see, Earth is not perfectly round. It's actually an oblate spheroid, meaning it's fatter at the equator and flatter at the poles. The bulge is caused by the Earth spinning on its axis.

Once you know where to look for knowledge, you need keen thinking skills to discover all you can from these sources. How can you learn from the world around you? How can you get the most from one of the best knowledge sources — books? Developing the discovery skill will not only fill your brain with new ideas, you'll also learn how to dig deep to get the most information.

Discovery: hot on the trail of the how, where, and why!

You've finally convinced your family to go camping this summer, so you want everything to go just right. First you pull out the map of the state parks your mom picked up at the local visitor center. You study the different campgrounds and choose one on a lake so you can bring the kayak. You go online and reserve the best campsite. As you get closer to the date, you visit the Internet site for weather forecasts so everyone knows what gear to bring. The morning of the trip, you use your handy manual of knots to help your dad tie the kayak onto the car. Way to go! Your awesome knowledge-discovery skills have assured a perfect vacation of outdoor fun. Your family may have such a great time, they'll want to go camping every year!

Crater Lake, which is in southern Oregon, is the deepest lake in the United States. It goes down 1,932 feet, so I hope you brought a lot of fishing line.

How could the skill of discovery come in handy in these situations?

* Your friends can't agree on the rules for a soccer game.
* You think a hamster would be a really cute pet, but you don't know what's involved in taking care of one.
* This winter has been unusually stormy and you wonder why.

Now you try it!

See what happens when you …

* read a *nonfiction* book (a true story).
* search the Internet for a topic you've always been curious about (hurricanes, tarantulas, whipped cream).
* ask someone to tell you about her job or hobby.

> "Not to know is bad; not to wish to know is worse."
> —Nigerian proverb

Getting the most from knowledge sources!

Have you ever had this experience? You're reading along in your book, and suddenly you realize you can't remember a thing you just read. You look back at the previous paragraphs and they don't even look familiar! That's because reading is not just about saying the words in your mind or looking at them printed on the page. It's about really understanding.

Good readers think about what they read while they're reading it. They realize when their understanding breaks down, and they stop and do something about it. They use thinking skills to make the words come alive and make sense. It's as if they are having a conversation with the book. You can talk to your books, too!

Here are three important thinking skills you can use to get the most from what you read. These same skills are also useful anytime you are taking in information — when you're visiting a web site, listening to your teacher explain something, watching a learning television show like a nature channel, or listening to a tour guide, for example.

Make connections. Connect the new information you learn to something you already know. Ask yourself how what you're reading about is the same as, or different from, something else you are familiar with. This makes the information more meaningful to you. Make as many connections as you can to help you understand and remember what you read. Use the phrases in red below as an easy way to make these powerful connections.

So let's say you read the sentence: *Tough skin protects an elephant from insect bites.* **Connect that fact to ...**

your life		the world	other books
That reminds me of **how my jacket protects me from the cold.**	That's different from me. I need to use insect repellent.	That's the same idea as **the bark protecting the tree trunk from forest fire.**	I remember reading about how some insects suck blood from animals.

Find the BIG ideas. You read a lot of information — too much to remember every word. It helps to *summarize*, or pull out the ideas that are most important. So after reading a half page or so, stop and ask yourself, "What was that about?" See if you can say the big idea to yourself in your own words, and in just a few sentences, before you read on.

Ask questions. As you read, think of other things you'd like to know about the topic and look for the answers. This skill makes you an "active reader." It's as if you are testing yourself as you read along to see if you are really paying attention and understanding what you read. You are also giving yourself a reason to read — wanting to find something out.

CHAT WITH YOUR BOOKS

Use bookmarks like the ones shown here to have conversations with your books while you read. Cut corners from old envelopes (a great way to use up junk-mail envelopes!). Use them to jot down your big ideas (mark with a light bulb), connections (a few links of chain), and questions (big question mark); then slip them onto the page corners. You'll find reading is fun and fascinating when you "talk to" your book, *and* you'll also deepen your understanding.

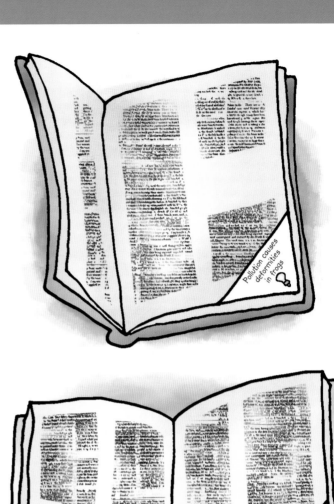

Dr. Elisabeth Kalko:
exploring the diversity of the tropical rain forest!

Dr. Elisabeth Kalko (left) and and a student weigh a bat during the JASON Project's expedition to Panama.

> "Although the job of a scientist is hard work, I love what I do ... I encourage my students to pursue what they love so they will enjoy what they do in the future."
>
> —Dr. Elisabeth Kalko

When she was growing up, Elisabeth Kalko was fascinated by animals and how they live. She wondered why some animals become extinct and whether people's behavior changes the way animals live. She studied science in school, always asking questions. She became a biologist to discover more answers. One day, Dr. Kalko was invited to join a science safari to the Mediterranean Sea. There she got the chance to study bats — not from books, but by observing real, live bats!

Thanks to that experience, Dr. Kalko developed a lifelong interest in these flying mammals. In their research, she and her team of scientists ask questions such as what do bats eat, how do they find their food, and how do they live with other bats. To find answers, the researchers sometimes use radio tracking: they outfit the bats with small, lightweight transmitters. By picking up signals, they follow bats through the forest. Their studies have taught people that bats are not ugly, scary creatures. As important members of the *ecosystem* (a natural area where particular plants and animals live together), bats are helpful, pollinating plants and eating harmful insects, for example. Dr. Kalko's passion for knowledge led her to make some key discoveries, including a new species of bat in Panama!

Dr. Kalko is now the head of the Department of Experimental Ecology at the University of Ulm, Germany, and a Staff Scientist at the Smithsonian Tropical Research Institute in Panama. She has been a host researcher for the JASON Project, where she led a team of students and teachers into the rain forests of Panama to promote better understanding of the importance of preserving these wonderful ecosystems. "I love the diversity I find in the Panamanian rain forest," says Dr. Kalko, "It allows me to make new discoveries every time I return."

Sharing what you know

EXCHANGING IDEAS WITH OTHERS

Once you're a knowledge-getter, you're ready to be a knowledge-giver, too. What do you know how to do: speak more than one language, play a sport, or draw action figures? What is a passionate interest of yours — horses, hockey, or astronomy? You're an expert on so many things that other people would love to know about.

How can you develop the *knowledge-sharing* skill? Just talking with people is one way. Have fun sharing your ideas and discoveries with your friends, your family, and your teachers. Do they find the same ideas interesting? Do they ask more questions about things you hadn't thought of? This learning give-and-take fires up your brain and only leads to wanting to know more. And think about all the other ways knowledge is shared: in books, on web sites, on television shows, in newspapers.

Share what you know and you'll find that people will be so grateful. That's because knowledge is such a valuable gift!

> **Sharing means ...** using something along with others.

The largest hailstone ever recorded fell in Coffeyville, Kansas, on September 3rd, 1979. It weighed in at 1.67 pounds.

Giving the gift of knowledge

You're working on the computer when you overhear your grandma saying how she has trouble staying in touch with her grandchildren. Suddenly you realize you've never seen her use the computer your dad gave her. You call her over and show her how you use your e-mail. She's amazed how great it works, but she doesn't even know how to set up an account, let alone send a message. You've never thought of yourself as an expert in anything, but here's Grandma calling you a "computer whiz"! You offer to give her a few lessons. And in no time at all, she's out there in cyberspace, instant messaging you and all your cousins!

How could knowledge-sharing skills make a difference in these situations?

* A nearby museum is looking for student volunteers to be tour guides for the new exhibit on rodents. You've had several hamsters and right now you have a guinea pig.
* Your little sister has trouble reading her history book. She just doesn't want to do her homework.
* Your mom wants to remodel the bathroom with new floor tile and is trying to figure out how much to buy. You remember what you learned in geometry about calculating area.

Now you try it!

See what happens when you …
* teach someone something you know how to do, such as shoot baskets, origami, or burn a CD of favorite songs.
* share an interesting discussion you had at school with your family at the dinner table.
* help a friend with an assignment in a subject you really enjoy.

Tim Berners-Lee:
creator of a worldwide system for sharing knowledge!

Tim Berners-Lee is the inventor of the World Wide Web, the Internet-based system for global information sharing. As the director of World Wide Web Consortium, he works to lead the Web to its full potential.

Search a topic on the Internet from baboons to tornados and you'll find more sites than you can possibly visit. So, who invented the Internet? There really was no one inventor. This global network of computers was originally created in the 1960s by many computer scientists as a way to link university and government computers. At first, computers used so many different kinds of operating systems and programs that, although they were linked by wires and cables, they couldn't understand each other. Computer scientist Tim Berners-Lee tackled this problem. In 1989, he figured out how computers that were linked via the Internet could communicate to share information, using http, a *protocol* (what determines how data is transferred between computers), and HTML, the language that displays the data on your computer screen. He named this web of computers — you guessed it — the World Wide Web.

Berners-Lee founded the World Wide Web Consortium (W3C), an organization dedicated to making the Web the best possible technology for sharing knowledge. He says it's "like a club of people and companies who feel the Web is important, and making it even better and even more powerful is important … thousands of people are now working on all kinds of wonderful things."

Thanks to the work of computer scientists like Tim Berners-Lee, people can explore, exchange, and develop ideas together, even if they are separated by vast distances. The World Wide Web has become one of the most powerful tools for the discovery and sharing of knowledge in human history!

"The Web is a tool for communicating … Let's use the Web to create neat new things. Let's use the Web to help people understand each other."
—Tim Berners-Lee

You're on the air!

Turn on the TV and you'll find how-to shows on cooking, home repair, motorcycle building, and more. With your friends, act out a knowledge-giving TV show of your own. Show your audience whatever you are an expert at: yo-yoing, making fudge, or drawing cartoon characters. Invite the live audience to ask questions or even to step into the TV "studio" to give it a try.

Or, make this episode a learning show about a topic or people of interest. Interview people who are experts on the things that fascinate them — tsunamis, amphibians, or Native American jewelry. Or, role-play famous people alive now or from history. Read the biography of a historical figure who interests you — Jane Goodall, Albert Einstein, Jesse Owens, or Leonardo da Vinci, for example. Then dress up as the person and use props for the interview. Your guests can even interact and discuss issues from their point of view. Take turns playing the parts of guest, talk-show host, and audience member. Videotape the shows and share them among friends and at school!

> "Give a man a fish and you feed him for a day. Teach a man to fish and you feed him for a lifetime."
> —Chinese proverb

Create a Kids' Yellow Pages

Where do folks look when they need help? In the Yellow Pages, of course. There you'll find experts who can help you with just about everything from how to choose new soccer cleats to what to feed your guppy.

Get your friends together and brainstorm the many different ways all of you are experts. Now share that knowledge! On separate sheets of paper, each of you explains your skills. Include photos and drawings. Then alphabetize all the pages, place them in a binder, and you've got a *Kids' Yellow Pages*! Make copies for everyone. So how can you learn to build a web page or make wonton soup? Check the *Kids' Yellow Pages*!

Enthusiasm

EAGERNESS TO KNOW

You know that excitement you feel when you finally "get it," whether it's a dance move, a math concept, or a goal-scoring play on the soccer field? Learning is a thrill. It's knowing about anything from volcanoes to vultures. It's knowing how to do anything from playing the bongos to building a robot. The more eager you are to learn, the more you will learn. And that enthusiasm is contagious. That means when you've got it, other kids catch the excitement from you. They want to learn, too!

So how can you become excited about learning? It's all about your attitude. Dale Carnegie was an author who made it his job to help people become enthusiastic. He said, "Act enthusiastic and you will be enthusiastic!" Give it a try. When you bring the *enthusiasm* skill to learning, you're on your way to developing the going after knowledge trait and achieving your goals.

> **Enthusiasm means ...** having a passionate interest or eagerness to know or do something.

Enthusiasm turns things around!

Your parents want to visit the famous art museum in the city where you're vacationing. You're dreading spending hours looking at a lot of paintings. Then your dad says he's hoping you'll help your younger brother have a good time at the museum because he's never visited one before. Uh-oh! Now you can't even act as bored as you're sure you're going to be!

OK, so you might as well act enthusiastic. You think of ways to make the visit like a game. You ask your brother to see if he can find a particular shape or color in each painting. Next you take turns telling the story or feeling you think a painting might be about. Then you try to see if either of you can pick your mom's favorite item on display in each gallery. Before you know it, you are both having fun!

BLUES BOY circa 2006

Remember, enthusiasm is contagious, so if you show an interest, others will, too! How could a little enthusiasm turn these situations around?

* You see a sign announcing underground caverns ahead on a road trip. Your parents hadn't planned to stop, but you've been reading about stalactites and stalagmites and it would be so cool to see the real thing.
* You are assigned a group project and there's just no energy on the team. Some members of the group say the topic is boring.
* The math lesson on percentages seems dull, but then you realize the concepts might actually help you shop around and get the best sale price on that new MP3 player you've been wanting.

Now you try it!

See what happens when you …
* get someone else excited about a great book you just read.
* tackle a skill that you've found challenging or frustrating, saying to yourself I *know* I can do this!
* play learning games such as Scrabble, checkers, or twenty questions with your family or a group of friends.

But I just don't find this interesting ...

When you're struggling to learn something that you don't find all that fun or fascinating, try these tips to help you approach the topic or activity with an open mind and discover its value.

Know "why." Ask your teacher why this information is important to know. Sometimes it's a skill or concept that you need to understand first in order to apply it to something more difficult and exciting — like learning about trajectory and then getting to design a rocket or hit more home runs.

Apply it to the real world. Look for examples of how you would use this information or skill in the real world. Might the learning help you do a better job of building, making, or cooking something? Making a purchase or saving money? Protecting yourself or the environment?

Know "how." Sometimes you're developing thinking skills rather than learning specific information. For example, you might be learning how to solve a problem or how to dig for the most information possible (see Getting the Most from Knowledge Sources, page 84).

The future is <u>now</u>. It may not help to hear adults say, "You'll appreciate knowing this when you're older," but sometimes it's true. When you become an adult voter trying to pick the best candidate (or *be* the best candidate!), you'll likely think, "I'm glad I learned all I could about democracy and how our government works." Or, if you become a structural engineer evaluating the load capacity of a bridge, you'll say to yourself, "All those years of studying math were sure worth it!"

> **"T**here is no knowledge that is not power."
>
> —Ralph Waldo Emerson, essayist and poet

Who needs math? Why should I care about numbers, and multiplying and amounts and totals and percentages?

And your allowance.

Never mind.

HOST A LEARNING CELEBRATION

It's not hard to be enthusiastic when you're partying with your friends, so invite them to a gathering where the learning is all fun and games! You could host a Book-Lovers Bash, an "Arty" Party, or this special Science Celebration.

Send Out Mysterious Invites!

On the invitations, leave a key word blank (your name, your guest's name, or the word "party," for example). Write the word later by dipping a toothpick or cotton swab into "invisible ink" (milk or lemon juice). This is a crude ink, but it does work. Instruct the reader to warm the paper near a lightbulb or other heat source to see the mystery word appear!

DOUBLE THE STRIP AND GLUE THE EDGES TOGETHER.

GATHER AT THE CENTER AND GLUE A PAPER STRIP AROUND THE GATHER.

INSERT AN ELASTIC CORD AND TIE IT AROUND YOUR NECK.

You are invited to a special _____ at my house on Friday. Be sure to bring a _____ just for fun!

Go for the "Science Lab" Look!

Round up adult-size white dress shirts from a thrift store. Cut them to look like lab coats. Place memo pads and mechanical pencils in the pockets. Hand out safety goggles. Offer your guests a 6" x 12" (15 x 30 cm) strip of crepe paper, glue, and an elastic cord so they can make bowties as shown.

Phweeee!

Pass Out Party Horns!

Pinch the end of a soda straw. Cut the corners to form a dull point. Place the cut end in your mouth. Blow, adjusting your hold, until you make a noise. What happens when you snip the straws to make party horns in all different lengths?

Have a Hovercraft Race!

Before the party, have an adult cut the necks from plastic soda and water bottles. Offer your guest scientists all sorts of lightweight containers: paper plates, clean deli tubs, food trays, and plastic lids. Punch or cut a hole in the center of your chosen container. Then, use lots of masking tape to seal the bottle neck in place over the hole. Set the hovercraft on a smooth surface and blow through the neck. Which hovercraft moves the farthest? Hovers the longest?

Try taping a 2" (5 cm) skirt onto the bottom edge of the container to create more of an air cushion. How does the hovercraft move now?

"Dancing" Drinks

Serve each scientist a glass of bubbly soda. Have them add a small handful of raisins to their glass. Watch the raisins dance. Why? Soda is filled with carbon dioxide bubbles that cling to the raisins and lift them to the surface. When the bubbles burst, the raisins sink to the bottom. There they collect new bubbles and the dance goes on.

Serve Baked Ice Cream

Impossible? Not so. Smart scientists know how to whip up a coating of protective (and edible!) bubbles so the ice cream won't melt in the oven.

Before guests arrive, spread ice cream onto thick, flat cookies. Freeze hard for about an hour. Have the scientists help make meringue (see recipe below). Each scientist spreads a thick coat of the meringue all over the cookie-and-ice-cream treat. No bare spots! Preheat oven to 425°F (220°C). Bake on a cookie sheet for about 8 to 10 minutes, or until meringue is lightly browned. Serve at once.

Meringue

In a bowl, use an electric mixer to beat 8 egg whites with ⅛ teaspoon (.5 ml) cream of tartar until foamy. Add a cup (250 ml) of powdered sugar, about a tablespoon (15 ml) at a time. Keep beating until the foam is stiff enough to stand up in little peaks. Remember, you need all those bubbles. The meringue's tiny air spaces will slow the oven heat from reaching the ice cream, just as your puffy winter jacket keeps your body heat in and the cold air out!

More Party Fun!

For more activities, games and treats, check out *Gizmos and Gadgets: Creating Science Contraptions That Work and Knowing Why* and *Super Science Concoctions: 50 Mysterious Mixtures for Fabulous Fun* both by Jill Frankel Hauser.

"**N**othing great was ever achieved without enthusiasm."
—Ralph Waldo Emerson, essayist and poet

Learning on your own

YOU'RE IN CHARGE!

Think of learning as an ongoing journey of discovery. Who's navigating? *You* are, if you are a "self-guided learner," meaning someone who takes charge of his or her own learning. You learn because you want to, not because you have to. You wonder why, and you follow up on your wonderings. You are interested, and you go after your interests. Does this mean you need to curl up with your math textbook every night before bed? If you like crunching numbers and puzzling out problems, then sure, go for it! Other activities could range from reading about reptiles or space travel to tinkering with a chemistry set to trying your hand at origami or woodworking.

When you take responsibility for your own learning, you become your own teacher. Developing the skill of *learning on your own* can happen anywhere and anytime. It can be as easy as grabbing a crossword puzzle book to keep busy on a long car trip or filling a spare hour by watching an awesome nature show on TV. This self-guided journey of discovery will help you do your best not only in school but throughout your life.

> **Learning on your own means ...** taking charge of going after knowledge.

Self-guided learning: What does it look like?

Your friends invite you to hear their band. They sound great! You wish you could play an instrument and join the group. You've always wanted to learn the guitar. How can you make it happen? First of all, you need a guitar. Hey, there's that one that's always sitting in the corner of your uncle's basement. You're sure he'll loan it to you just to get started. Now, how to play the thing? Well, there's your uncle. And your friends in the band might show you a thing or two. You discover sites on the Internet that teach chords. You go to the library and find some awesome how-to-play-guitar books. There's even a learning DVD. After a few weeks, you can play a few songs. Now you just need a commitment to practice and a goal to join the band!

How could taking charge of your own learning make you the ultimate knowledge-getter in these situations?

* Your friend is really into boa constrictors. So how do they capture their prey?
* A techno-expo is being held in your community. Admission is free.
* Your dad is complaining about the family's energy bill. The power company is offering a free brochure on household energy-saving tips.

Now you try it!

See what happens when you …

* watch a documentary on a topic that you have always wanted to know more about.
* borrow or check out a how-to book and follow the directions to make a craft or learn a skill.
* keep a journal where every week you write down the meaning of one new, cool word that you hear or read.

wiseacre (WIZE-ay-kuhr)
One who obnoxiously pretends to be wise; smart aleck; wise guy.

Yo-Yo Ma:
a lifelong journey of musical discovery

World-famous cellist Yo-Yo Ma began playing the cello at age 4. He is always experimenting with different musical styles in his ongoing search for new ways to interpret music for his audiences.

Yo-Yo Ma is a world-famous cellist. Born in France to Chinese parents, he grew up in the United States. At age 4, he began studying the cello, and he performed in a concert on television when he was 8 years old. As a kid, Ma didn't like to practice, but he knew he had to in order to become the best musician he could be.

Just because Ma is considered one of finest performers of classical music in the world doesn't mean he has stopped learning anything new. His curiosity leads him to explore all kinds of musical styles. Ma has performed American bluegrass music, Chinese melodies, Argentinean tangos, Brazilian rhythms, New Age music, and jazz. Through his Silk Road Project, the world has heard him reinvent traditional music from countries along ancient Asian trade routes. He has made movie soundtracks. Ma has even performed for the muppets on *Sesame Street*.

What has Ma learned by exploring so many different kinds of music? He says, "It took me way beyond what I knew, into places of which I was totally scared, but as I became less frightened, I welcomed new ways of thinking and approaching something. It made me an infinitely richer person, and I think a better musician." Yo-Yo Ma's passion to keep on learning has made the world a richer place musically for all of us, too!

> "I've been traveling all over the world for 25 years, performing, talking to people, studying their cultures and musical instruments, and I always come away with more questions in my head than can be answered."
>
> —Yo-Yo Ma

READY-TO-GO LEARNING KITS!

Whatever your interest, you can assemble a special learning kit by gathering supplies in a cool backpack or other easy-to-carry bag so you are always ready to set off on a journey of discovery. Make one kit — or make them all!

Unlock-Your-Creativity Kit

Let your imagination soar as you create amazing artistic creations, from collages and sketches to jewelry, mini-sculpture, and more!

- Colored pencils and markers
- Sketch pad
- Beads
- String, embroidery floss, or colored wire
- Pipe cleaners
- Scissors
- Magazine with cool pictures to cut out
- Glue stick
- Glitter
- Creative Clay in a ziplock bag (see recipe below)

> "Teachers open the door. You enter by yourself."
> —Chinese proverb

Creative Clay

In a pan, combine all the ingredients: 2 cups (500 ml) flour, 2 cups (500 ml) water, 1 cup (250 ml) salt, 1 tablespoon (15 ml) cream of tartar, and 2 tablespoons (30 ml) cooking oil. Cook over low heat, stirring all the time until the mixture looks like mashed potatoes.

Set the cooled glob on a floured surface and knead the dough until smooth. Add food coloring or glitter if you like.

Super Science Kit

With these simple supplies, you'll be prepared to carefully observe and explore the world, just as scientists do.

- Hand lens or eye loop
- Small clear plastic containers for specimens
- Plastic spoons
- Flashlight
- Observation journal
- Insect Vacuum Collector (see below)
- Insect field guide

Insect Vacuum Collector

Have an adult poke a hole through the lid and bottom of a clear film canister. Insert half a drinking straw into each hole and complete the collector as shown.

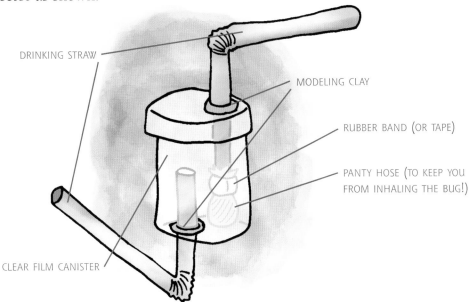

DRINKING STRAW

MODELING CLAY

RUBBER BAND (OR TAPE)

PANTY HOSE (TO KEEP YOU FROM INHALING THE BUG!)

CLEAR FILM CANISTER

> "The good life is one inspired by love and guided by knowledge."
> —Bertrand Russell, mathematician and philosopher

Holding the collector sideways, point it at an insect tiny enough to fit easily through the straw at the bottom. Suck through the straw at the top with the covering and the insect will land in the canister. Observe awhile. Then release your tiny specimen back to its home.

Always-Ready-to-Read Kit

Always be in the middle of reading a great book. All you need in your reading kit is a terrific book and a bookmark (page 85) to hold your place! Would you like some reading recommendations? Ask your friends what they are reading. Teachers, parents, and librarians will also have great ideas. Be sure to check these lists for award-winners, too (see RESOURCES, page 124).

Joining

No matter where we live, we are not alone. As part of our daily lives, we work, play, and learn with other people. We can get so much more accomplished — not to mention that things go a lot more smoothly — when we get along with each other and work together. Think of it as being on a team — a sports team, for example. Every member has a job. Maybe yours is to guard a base, move the ball farther down the field, or protect another player so she can score. The point is no one person wins the game. Everyone does his or her part and works together to accomplish the goal. Now that's team spirit!

Any group of people can be a team: your family, your friends, your schoolmates, your neighborhood, your country, or even all the people in the world! So whether you pitch in to help your family with yard work or your country pitches in to help another nation rebuild after a tornado, that's teamwork in action. People working together can accomplish amazing goals not possible to achieve when each works alone.

You won't be too surprised to learn that the trait of joing together takes good "people skills," qualities that mean you care about, respect, and

Together!

TEAMING UP WITH OTHERS TO MAKE A DIFFERENCE

work readily with others. Let's see what they are:

Caring. You think about others. You are considerate of how they feel and want to do your part to help when they're in trouble.

Respect. You accept and value other people. You treat them fairly even if they are different from you.

Cooperation. You work with others to achieve a goal that's best for everyone.

Problem-solving. You share your thinking to come up with the best solution for everyone.

Citizenship. You take responsibility for being part of a *community* (a group of people with something in common) and are willing to act for the good of that community.

Of course, developing your ability to join together with others means you'll need to work with other people. To practice the skills in this chapter, gather your friends and family. You'll accomplish all sorts of things, big and small. Learning to be a team player makes you a stronger individual, too. And being part of a team effort strengthens your community, whether it's your school, your block, or your town, and makes it a better place!

Caring

CONSIDERATION AND COMPASSION FOR OTHERS

Caring means ...
showing concern for others.

Think about some of the caring things people have done for you. How did they make you feel? You have the power to share that same wonderful feeling with others. You can spread happiness through acts of kindness and thoughtfulness. What could you do? Sometimes it's as simple as being a good listener or giving someone a compliment. Maybe you could offer to help someone with your time or skills. Or, you could get involved in a community project helping people in need.

Compassion is an ingredient of caring. It means you think about how others feel by putting yourself in their place, especially when they are going through a difficult time. Then you do something to help. Another ingredient is consideration. That means you take into account the needs and feeling of others. If you really consider how your

actions affect others, you won't be cruel or hurtful. When you treat people with the same kindness and generosity you value, most likely they'll treat you kindly in return.

Caring connects us with other people. It creates a strong community where each person is concerned about the others. That's why caring is such a powerful character skill for joining together with others.

A little consideration goes a long way

Tuesday mornings are really hectic in your house. You have to be at school 45 minutes early for band practice, so your mom gives you a ride on her way to work. Tuesday is also trash/recycling pickup day so she is always rushing to get the containers out by the curb before the truck goes by. It's embarrassing to always rush into rehearsal late, but you don't seem to be able to get out of the house on time. How could this situation improve if you showed a little consideration? What if you got up a few minutes earlier so you could take care of the trash for her? Or, fix your own lunch (if you don't already) and while you're at it, offer to fix your mom's lunch, too! The morning will go more smoothly and you'll be in the band room right on time. Your mom will be in a great mood, too!

Think about ways an act of consideration or compassion could change these other situations.

* You see your elderly neighbor struggling to clear the heavy snow off his path.
* Your teacher sprained her wrist and needs some help in her classroom putting things away at the end of the day.
* Your brother is really struggling with his math homework. You remember when math seemed hard for you, too. Now you feel pretty confident about it.
* You hear about a school on the coast that lost its library in a hurricane.

I'll take care of the plants, Mom!

> "**W**e are not put on this Earth to see through one another, but to see one another through."
> —anonymous

Now you try it!

See what happens when you …

* compliment three people during the day.
* ask, "How's it going?" Then stop and really listen to the answer.
* do a chore someone else usually does, like sweep the floor or water the plants.

Chi Nguyen:
showing compassion for impoverished children

Chi Nguyen gets a hug from Hong, age 8, at Dieu Giac Orphanage in Vietnam.

"**T**hese kids have endured more than I can imagine and yet they manage to sustain such optimism. Each of these children deserves an opportunity for a better life."

—Chi Nguyen

Growing up in California, Chi Nguyen knew there were children in the world who lived in extreme poverty. Her parents had shared stories of the history of Vietnam, where they had grown up. They told her how children still live there today without enough food, clothing, or a decent place to live.

Chi felt sympathy for these impoverished children. But she took one more step that made her compassionate — she took action to help them. In 1998, 10-year-old Chi and her sister, Truc, began raising money. Chi started by selling her personal collection of Beanie Babies along with homemade toffee. She raised more than $1,000 in one day!

The following summer, Chi traveled to the village of Giai Xuan in Vietnam, where her donation had helped build a library. She also visited the village of Can Tho, where she met orphaned children who lived on the streets. She believed that the best hope to bring them out of poverty was through education. So Chi and Truc organized more fund-raisers to help these children go to school. With their friends, they held concerts featuring their musical talents. Working with Viet Nam Health Education and Literature Projects (VNHELP), Chi and Truc have raised more than $65,000 to provide clothing, meals, education, and medical aid for Vietnamese orphans.

World poverty can seem like too big of a problem to do anything about. But Chi felt such compassion for these kids that she took on their cause and worked with others to help them. "I have to start helping wherever I can," she says, "and I feel very close to the children in Can Tho." Just look at all she has accomplished so far!

CARE BAR

Put a smile on someone's face with this sweet treat bearing its special message! These bars are perfect for fund-raisers, too. Create a label that names your cause: *Endangered Species Bar, End Poverty Bar, Clean Planet Bar,* for example. Share information about your project on the label as well.

What you need

- Candy bar with outer paper wrapper and inner foil wrapper
- Scissors
- Paper
- Fine-tip markers, colored pencils, or a computer
- Glue stick

What you do

1 Carefully remove the paper wrapper from the candy bar. Keep the foil wrapper in place. Using the paper wrapper as a template, cut a piece of blank paper the same size.

2 Create a message about something happening in the life of the recipient: *Get Well, Good Luck, Congratulations, Happy Birthday, Friends Forever.* Use the markers or colored pencils to decorate the new paper wrapper. Or, use the computer to create the wrapper. You can download images or scan personal photos, and write messages with fancy fonts.

3 Fold the wrapper around the bar. Use a glue stick to connect the edges of the new wrapper.

> "No man is an island entire of itself; every man is a piece of the continent, a part of the main."
> —John Donne, poet

KINDNESS STICK'EMS

On a large-sized pad of self-stick notes, write a kind message such as, *I'm so lucky to have you as a friend.* Then draw a small sketch to match the message, such as you and your friend each holding a four-leaf clover. Sign your name. These notes are safe to stick anywhere — on a computer screen, backpack, desk, or mug, inside a locker, or in a lunch box. How about on the page of math problems that your friend has for homework tonight? Use your mini–art pad to create many more messages and spread kindness as you go through your day.

Respect
ACCEPTING AND VALUING DIFFERENCES

There are more than six billion people on Earth. But there isn't any other person just like you. In fact, no two people are alike. People have so many beautiful colors of skin, hair, and eyes. Our bodies differ in size and shape. We are born all over the world into different cultures and we speak many languages. We also live our lives in so many different ways.

All this diversity makes the world a fascinating place! But it has its challenges, too. You know how you can feel when you strongly disagree with someone. *Respect* begins with accepting people who may be

different than you and being willing to consider ideas that don't reflect what you personally believe. It's not about lumping people together in a group — by their looks, their religion, or where they were born. It means valuing them for who they are inside. Remember, every person is unique. So, we see people as individuals and follow the familiar Golden Rule: treat each other the way we want to be treated ourselves.

While respect can mean acceptance of ideas from around the world, it's also about acceptance right here at home. It means going along with your mom's insistence on quiet after 9 P.M., tolerating your friend's love for peanut butter on hot dogs, or accepting the kid in your class who dresses in a way that the other students don't think is cool. Does respect mean that all behaviors are accepted? Of course not! Cruelty, disrespect, or violence, for example, are never OK.

It may feel more comfortable to hang out with kids who are like you. But getting to know someone who is different is a great way to learn about new places, foods, music, and more! And who knows, you might even discover a new outlook on the world as you make a new friend. Respect and openness to new ideas give you that opportunity. And best of all, you're doing your part to make the world a peaceful place where everyone feels accepted!

Spreading acceptance and respect!

The bell rings and you're off to class. The group of girls you're with snicker as Magda walks by. "Look at those funny clothes she wears," says Kayla. "I've heard she dresses that way because her family believes weird stuff. They're not our religion, you know." "Yeah," Alyssa adds, "My dad says people like that should go back to their own country."

You've noticed Magda, too — how she is always by herself. You know it's not fun to be lonely. Encouraging your friends to be more accepting would help Magda feel welcome in your school. What if you spoke up, "Hey, our country is great because most everyone has come from somewhere else!" Or, "I think it would be interesting to find out more about Magda." Or just, "Whoa, do you guys know how mean you sound? I know you and you aren't mean people! Come on, let's say hi to her at recess."

Often, people are afraid or suspicious of things just because they're unfamiliar. Strike up a conversation with Magda on the playground and your friends might see that that "weird stuff" isn't so weird after all. Accepting others for who they are not only spreads kindness, it builds team spirit in a community as well.

Think about ways respect and acceptance could change these other situations:

* A group of kids is spreading the word not to go to Marquis's birthday party because he's "not cool."
* You look forward to Friday night pizza, but your mom wants to try the new Thai restaurant in town. A couple of your friends said the food is too spicy.
* Gabriella comes to your school from Ecuador. She speaks very little English and it takes her forever to ask the teacher a question in class. You see her struggling with her homework in the library.

> "**S**hare our similarities, celebrate our differences."
> —M. Scott Peck, author

Now you try it!

Learn about a country, religion, or culture different from yours by searching the Internet for activities and information (see RESOURCES, page 124)! See what happens when you …

* make a new friend by writing to a pen pal.
* try a recipe from a different country and serve it to family or friends.
* learn some phrases in different languages. Try them out on your teacher and your classmates or on your family!

FRIENDSHIP TRIANGLE BOOK

Think about a good friend of yours. In many ways you are alike. Yet in other ways, you are different. In any case, you are still friends who accept and value each other!

Create this friendship book together. On one side of the paper strip, fill each triangle page with ways you and your friend are alike. On the back side of the paper strip, fill each triangle page with ways you are different.

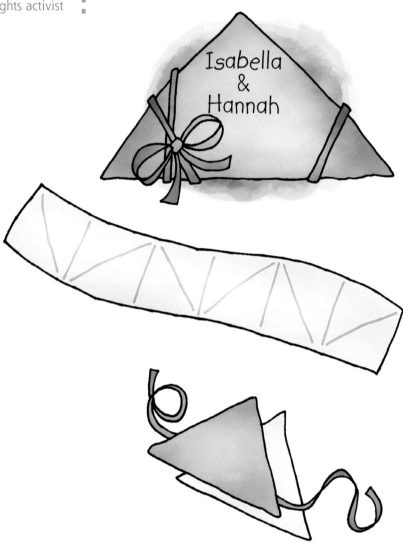

Isabella
&
Hannah

What you need
- Sheet of paper
- Scissors
- Tape
- Construction paper
- 14" (35 cm) of narrow ribbon
- Glue

What you do

1 Fold the sheet of paper in half the long way and cut along the fold line. Tape the sections together to make a long strip. Accordion-fold the strip to form small triangles as shown.

2 From the construction paper, cut two covers slightly larger than the triangle. Insert the ribbon between the top cover and the first page as shown and glue that cover to the page, pressing firmly to secure the ribbon. Glue on the back cover.

3 Once the book is dry, fill the pages. Tie the ribbon to hold the pages in place.

PLAY "WE ARE ALL ALIKE!"

Gather a group of friends for this active game that will remind everyone of how much we all have in common!

Place chairs in a circle. Use one less chair than the number of players. Everyone sits in a chair except one player who stands in the center. She calls out something like, "I like tacos better than hot dogs. We are all alike!" Anyone who agrees with the statement runs, along with the caller, across the circle to find a new seat (in other words, you can't pick the seat right next to where you were just sitting).

The person left standing goes in the center and makes the next statement. Statements might be, "I have older sisters ... I know how to skateboard ... I like (fill in the name of a favorite song, book, television program, or movie) ..." Players move after the words, "We are all alike!" At the end of the game, talk about how many times everyone had a chance to run. What does that say about our similarities and differences?

> "Put yourself in the other man's place and then you will know why he thinks certain things and does certain deeds."
> —Elbert Hubbard, philosopher and author

Cooperation

WORKING TOGETHER FOR A COMMON PURPOSE

Cooperation means ...
working with others to accomplish a goal.

Many jobs are just too big for one person to accomplish on his own. Imagine a canned-food drive where you are the only one who brings a few cans. That sure won't feed a needy family or fill the community food shelf. But say there are 600 students at your school, and everyone donates just one can. Now you're talking about groceries for many families! *Cooperation* is the skill of working together to solve differences or to achieve a goal.

What if you are willing to do your part, but you don't like the job you've been assigned? That's where compromise comes in. This important attitude is the key to cooperation. *Compromise* means finding a middle ground. Things might not go exactly your way, but it doesn't mean you give in completely, either. Let's say you and your sister hate taking out the trash. You'd both rather unload the groceries instead. You can compromise by taking turns doing both chores.

Experience the power of cooperation. See what amazing things happen when everyone chips in to do her part!

"Union gives strength."
—Aesop, author

Cooperation community-style!

The vacant land down the street is the only place in the neighborhood where kids can play and folks can walk, bike, and enjoy nature. You hear the city is considering selling it to a developer that wants to build a shopping center. You and your family complain to each other about it, but it seems impossible to change the situation.

Before you give up, however, think about all your neighbors who use that space. Maybe you could all work together to keep the land open. You could start by passing out flyers or making phone calls explaining to your neighbors how they could help. Families could write letters to the town council and to the local newspaper to say why that land is so important to the community and propose it become a community park. Folks could volunteer to clean it up and cut trails for everyone to enjoy. Sometimes it takes a whole neighborhood working together to accomplish a goal.

How could cooperation improve these other situations?

* Every player wants to be the one who shoots baskets and scores points. So, no one is doing defense. And players keep trying to make baskets from too far away. The team keeps losing.
* The principal has cut recess time because of the huge litter problem on the playground every day.
* You and your sisters all need to use the computer to get part of your homework finished, but there is only one in your house. Every afternoon there is a big argument about computer time.

Now you try it!

See what happens when …

* your family sits down together to talk about who does which chore and when.
* you compromise with a friend when you can't agree.
* you join a community, school, or youth group project aimed at making your community a better place.

"We are not going to be able to operate our Spaceship Earth successfully nor for much longer unless we see it as a whole spaceship and our fate as common. It has to be everybody or nobody."
—Buckminster Fuller, engineer

TEAM-BUILDING FUN & GAMES!

Everyone is a winner in these games — if everyone cooperates.

Before you start to play, get to know your teammates. Pair up and conduct mini-interviews (no more than five minutes). Then introduce your partner to the team in one minute or less. For more fun, listen for an interesting fact during the interview that no one would know about your partner. Write it on an index card and give it to the group leader. The leader reads the cards and the group must guess the mystery person.

Hoop-Go-Round

Place a hula hoop over one player's arm. That player then joins hands with at least five other players to form a circle.

Without letting go of hands, move the hula hoop around the circle. You'll discover you need the help of your teammates as each player wriggles through the hoop and moves it along.

⊚⁕⁎ More cooperative fun! ⁎⁕⊚

* Time how long it takes to send the hoop around. Now see if you can beat your time.
* See how many times the hoop can travel around in three minutes.
* Challenge another group to a Hoop-Go-Round race.
* See what happens when you add two or more hoops to the circle or vary the number of players.

Balloon Bop

At least five players hold hands in a circle. Without letting go of hands, how long can the group keep a balloon aloft? Use any parts of your body you like, just don't let go! Try some variations (see More Cooperative Fun! with Hoop-Go-Round above).

COOPERATIVE CIRCLES

Try these formations on a soft surface such as carpet or lawn.

* Hold hands in a circle. Move outward until arms are stretched, but grips are still firm. With feet in place, everyone slowly leans backwards. Now count off, 1, 2 around the circle. This time, the 1s lean forward while the 2s lean back.

* Drop hands and stand sideways. Place hands on each other's waists. Move close together so that each team member can sit on the knees of the person behind him (team members might need to adjust their positions). Plan and practice a few times. When the team gets good at this, try counting "1, 2, 3" and then everyone claps!

* Hold hands in a line. The leader coils the line into a tight circle. Now the person at the end of the line uncoils the line by coiling the line into a new circle. Everyone follows, trying not to break the line.

Cooperative flight

Have you ever wondered why geese fly in that magnificent V-shaped formation? It's teamwork in action! As each bird flaps its wings, it creates a lifting force for the bird that follows. This uplift allows the flock to fly 70% more efficiently than if each bird flew alone. The lead bird doesn't get the advantage of the uplift, so it rotates back after a while and another bird takes a turn at the head. The birds in the back honk to encourage the front birds to keep up the pace. With this cooperation and teamwork, some flocks of Canada geese migrate as far south as Mexico!

What lessons can we learn from this airborne team?

* We can make more progress when we work as a team and support each other.

* Everyone has an important job. Take turns, even in leadership.

Problem-solving

FINDING THE BEST SOLUTION

Problem-solving means ... figuring out a solution to a difficult situation.

Problems — we all face them in our daily lives. Some are huge, like the global warming story on the news last night. Some are simpler, like getting busy family members to their different destinations on time. Having good problem-solving skills makes you a very important team member. You've got what it takes to work out solutions and help solve problems big and small.

The skill of *problem-solving,* especially in a group, builds on many of the other skills that are right in this book! For starters, you need focus (see pages 36–39) so you can zero in on exactly what the issue is. Creative thinking (see pages 43–46) and resourcefulness (see pages 46–51) will help you develop solutions. Problem-solving also takes resilience (see pages 17–19) and perserverance (see pages 40–42), because the solution might not work the first time and you need to be ready to bounce right back and try something else.

Five steps to a solution

This five-step plan adapts to solving almost any problem, large or small. For a complex problem, you may need to take the time to work through each step. On the other hand, quickly thinking about a step or two may be all you need for a fresh outlook on a simple problem.

1. Understand the problem. Let everyone have a chance to state the problem as each sees it. Talk about what caused the problem. Combine everyone's viewpoint into a common understanding.

2. Brainstorm plans. Consider many possible ways to solve the problem, not just one or two ideas. Think about resources you already have to help solve the problem (people, time, money, skills) or determine what you need. Be open-minded as you consider everyone's ideas.

3. Pick the plan the group agrees is best. Think about the consequences of the plan. What might happen if you do this? Don't look for the easiest solution. Pick the one that best solves the problem for everyone.

4. Go for it! Put your plan into action. Figure out each step. Decide who will do each task. Estimate when each step will be finished.

5. Evaluate and make it better. How's it going? If it's not working quite right, make changes. Has something else happened as a result and you need a new plan? If so, start again. But this time you'll have learned something from what didn't work, so you'll be closer to a better solution.

"**A** problem is a chance for you to do your best."
—Duke Ellington, musician

The five-step plan in action!

Help! The dishwasher has broken down. It's time for you to come to the rescue with your problem-solving skills and put the FIVE STEPS TO A SOLUTION plan (see page 116) into action. First, you gather your family. Yes, everyone agrees the dishwasher can't handle another load, but A-1 Plumbing can't come until Wednesday of next week. Now, you all brainstorm solutions for what to do in the meantime: Let the dishes pile up, use paper plates, have Mom hand-wash the dishes, (hey, that's not fair!), or have everyone take turns washing the dishes. Then pick the best plan. Everyone agrees to take turns hand-washing dishes and help out clearing the table until Wednesday. Lastly, you gather everyone back together after a day or two. You agree that the plan is going well except for a few small glitches that require a little reworking — like Ethan can't wash on Monday night because of soccer practice. In fact with everyone pitching in, cleanup is going faster than usual!

> "How you think about a problem is more important than the problem itself — so always think positively."
> —Norman Vincent Peale, author

Use your problem-solving skills to find solutions to these situations.

* Your parents point out that you and your brother never seem to be around to walk the dog.
* The cafeteria line is so long, many kids are stuck waiting in line for almost their entire lunch period.
* Your mom asks you to babysit on the same night you've got plans with your friends.

The only bad ideas are the ones that kids fail to mention.

Now you try it!

See what happens when …
* your friends meet to talk about a problem that everyone's been complaining about.
* you brainstorm plans and try out the best one.
* you go back over the plan and figure out an even better solution!

Apollo 13:
problem-solving in outer space!

The *Apollo 13* crew of Fred Haise (left), Jack Swigert, and Jim Lovell pose on the day before launch.

"**B**e thankful for problems. If they were less difficult, someone with less ability might have your job."

—Jim Lovell

"Houston, we've had a problem." These words came from *Apollo 13* to Mission Control on April 13, 1970. They set off one of the most amazing problem-solving ventures in U.S. space-program history. Over 200,000 miles (333,000 km) from Earth, an explosion had ripped through the spaceship, threatening the safe return of the three astronauts on board.

The spacecraft had three parts: the command module for travel, the service module for storing supplies, and the lunar module for exploring the Moon. With the huge explosion, the crew watched their precious supply of oxygen gush out of the service module and into outer space. A fire had destroyed most of the command module's electrical systems so the crew was without water or power.

The original mission (the lunar landing) was abandoned, and hundreds of engineers on the ground immediately began figuring out how to bring the crew safely home. There were many problems to solve. The return path had to be redesigned. The three men had to move to the lunar module even though it only held enough water and oxygen to keep two men alive for two days. They had to save fuel for the return trip so they kept the temperature at 38°F (3°C).

Another problem was how to deal with the poisonous carbon dioxide exhaled by the men. Mission Control had to figure out a way using only the materials that would be aboard the module. Using plastic bags, cardboard notebook covers, and electrical tape, they solved the problem.

Four days later, the crew re-entered the command module. Moisture had formed on the controls. Were the wires behind the panels also wet and ruined? Was there enough fuel left to return? The incredible problem-solving skills of the crew and Mission Control paid off. After more than five days in space, the command module splashed safely down in the Pacific Ocean with three thankful astronauts aboard!

PROBLEM-SOLVING CHALLENGES

Crossing the Swamp

Your team must figure out a way to cross a "dangerous swamp." The only safe place to step is on stepping–stone paper plates you place ahead of yourself as you walk across. The team gets half as many plates as team members, so players don't have enough plates to get across and have to pick them up and reuse them as they go. Only one foot may be on a plate at a time. Clearly mark starting and ending lines. Use the five-step plan on page 116 to solve how you will move across the space. Hint: Some team members may need to cross back to help the rest of the team. Time your team to see how long it takes to bring everyone across the "swamp." Now try to beat your time using a different plan.

Nailing a Solution

Can your team figure out a way to balance nine nails on the head of a tenth one? Use the five-step plan (see page 116) to come up with a solution. You'll need 10 long, smooth, flathead nails for this challenge. Give up? See the solution below.

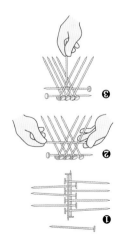

Nail Solution

1. Make a "nail sandwich" as shown.

2. Slowly lift the "sandwich" while holding the tips of the bottom nail "bun." The seven nails will slide together and their heads will lock against the top nail "bun."

3. Balance this on top of the tenth nail.

Citizenship

DOING YOUR PART FOR YOUR COMMUNITY

Citizenship means ... carrying out the rights and responsibilities that come with being a member of a community.

"Ask not what your country can do for you; ask what you can do for your country." Those words of former United States President John F. Kennedy summarize the responsibility of citizenship, no matter what country you live in.

Citizenship means honoring the *ideals* (see page 52) we value. It means taking responsibility to make sure your community is a place that carries out those ideals and guarantees that the basic rights are there for everyone. It includes obeying the laws that make the community fair and safe for everyone. In other words, it means doing your part to help make sure your community and your country are awesome places for adults and kids to live!

Practicing the skill of good *citizenship* is the perfect opportunity to put many of the other character skills you've been learning in this book into action. As an active, committed citizen, you put your beliefs to work to make a positive difference. You'll be building a strong community (your neighborhood, school, country, and the world!) while becoming the best person you can be!

Citizenship in action!

You know that protecting the Earth's resources is an important community ideal, and a personal ideal of yours as well. You hear on the news that your city needs to build a new landfill site to handle all its trash. You learned in science class that paper can be recycled and reused so that it does not end up in a landfill site. The next day at school you are about to throw your rough draft in the trash basket when you notice it's full of paper wads. You realize your school doesn't recycle paper! You talk about the problem in class. Other concerned students gather around you at morning break. You come up with a plan to start a paper-recycling project at your school. That's citizenship in action!

Think about how citizenship can come alive in these situations.

* The homeless shelter only gets enough volunteers to help serve meals during the winter holidays.
* A community member donates money to your class. Your teacher asks the students if they'd like to use the money to subscribe to a weekly news magazine for students or for a pizza party.
* Your dad asks if you'd like to go with him when he votes, but he's leaving right when your favorite television show starts.
* The city has posted a sign at the start of the river-walk trail: "All dogs must be leashed." But your dog loves to run free.

> "**H**e that does good to another does good also to himself."
> —Seneca, philosopher and playwright

Now you try it!

See what happens when …
* your family picks a news story to talk about at dinner.
* you join a service project or volunteer (see page 29) to improve your community.
* you ask one or two adults what citizenship means to them.

Martin Luther King, Jr.: the ultimate citizen

On August 28, 1963, Dr. Martin Luther King, Jr., delivered his famous "I Have a Dream" speech on the steps of the Lincoln Memorial at the Civil Rights March on Washington, D.C. The speech included these words: "I have a dream that one day this nation will rise up and live out the true meaning of its creed: 'We hold these truths to be self-evident that all men are created equal.'"

> "Life's most persistent and nagging question is 'What are you doing for others?'"
> —Martin Luther King, Jr.

Imagine you are forbidden from playing with your best friend because his skin is a different color than yours. You can't drink from the same water fountain, swim in the same pool, or attend the same school as people with lighter-colored skin. This was America when Martin Luther King, Jr., grew up in the 1930s and 1940s.

Dr. King was the ultimate citizen. He understood the great ideals upon which America was founded. He also recognized that these ideals were not applied fairly to everyone. He knew the Declaration of Independence said, "all men are created equal." So he was determined to make these words true by ending the injustice he saw around him.

Dr. King taught through peaceful marches and powerful speeches. He said that even if we look different from one another, we must still respect each other. He and many other people risked their homes, their jobs, and even their lives to make sure America honored its founding principles. Although Dr. King was a citizen-leader, and not an elected official, his leadership helped to change the way people treat each other and to create laws to protect the rights of all Americans. He devoted his life to public service and encouraged everyone to volunteer. The King Center in Atlanta, Georgia, founded by Dr. King's widow, Coretta Scott King, is dedicated to fulfilling his vision of community service and nonviolent social change.

A COMMUNITY-ACTION BLOG!

A *blog* (short for web log) is a site all your own that can be whatever you want it to be. There are already millions of blogs on the Web, on about every topic imaginable. What does blogging have to do with citizenship?

Well, if you feel passionate about an issue in your community, you can use a blog to post your ideas and get other people involved, too. You can educate people about your cause and invite them to join you in working on solutions. So when you have a concern, you can share it with a friend … or you can announce it on your blog, where your ideas could be read around the world!

Remember, blogs are public. Get an adult involved right from the start to be sure you are blogging safely.

Choose a host. Setting up a blog is easy (and free). First, find a host (see RESOURCES, page 124). You'll be guided through the steps of setting up an account, naming your blog, and choosing a template.

Create a look. Think about how you want your blog to look. Do you want text only? Do you want graphics or pictures? Ask your friends for suggestions. You may want to add music or videos to make your blog more inviting.

Share ideas. Your blog is a place where people come together to learn about your cause and offer suggestions. Create a section for them to post comments. Create another section where you offer solutions others can help with.

> **"B**e alert to give service. What counts a great deal in life is what we do for others."
>
> —anonymous

• •

Have you noticed a problem that no one seems to be working on? If you have an awesome idea for a solution, how about starting a project of your own? We've shared stories throughout this book about people who did just that — and there are so many more out there! Remember, every solution to a local, national, or even an international problem started with one person's idea. Why not yours?

Staying informed, sharing information, and doing your part to see that the community becomes the best it can be is what citizenship is all about! For more ideas on getting involved, see page 29 and RESOURCES, page 124.

Resources

These web sites and organizations will help you build the skills in this book. Web site addresses may change over time; if necessary, try searching under the organization's name. You'll find other great sites on the Web by entering the name of a trait or character skill from this book or by searching for the words suggested beneath each heading. Add the word *kid* or *teen* to find sites targeted just for you.

MAKING THE MOST OF WHO YOU ARE!

Search words: *character building, self-esteem*

BookEnds http://www.bookends.org
A nonprofit organization that recycles children's books through student-run book drives and places them in schools and with youth organizations in need; (818) 716-1198.

Canada's Guide to Healthy Eating and Physical Activity
http://www.phac-aspc.gc.ca/guide/index_e.html
Visit this site to obtain a copy of *Canada's Guide to Healthy Eating and Physical Activity* and other information on a healthy lifestyle.

The Cesar E. Chavez Foundation
http://www.cesarechavezfoundation.org/
Events, activities, and curriculum to promote the legacy of civil rights leader Cesar E. Chavez; (818) 265-0300.

Crossroads of Character http://library.thinkquest.org/J001675F
An interactive web site for learning about character and how to develop it.

Good character.com http://www.goodcharacter.com
Click on your grade level for character-building activities. Resources and materials for educators also.

KidsHealth http://kidshealth.org/index.html
Click on the *Kids Site* or the *Teens Site* for dealing with the feelings and the challenges of growing up. Resources for parents also.

Lance Armstrong Foundation http://www.livestrong.org
A nonprofit organization with the mission of inspiring and empowering people with cancer through education, advocacy, public health, and research programs.

USDA's MyPyramid.gov http://www.myPyramid.gov
Visit this site to obtain a copy of USDA's food pyramid plan and poster.

GETTING INVOLVED!

Search words: *kids, clubs,* along with the hobby, skill, craft, or sport you'd like to know more about; for example: *kids clubs skateboarding*

Children Helping Children http://www.childrenhelpingchildren.net
A New York–based charity organization that fund-raises nationally for medical charities and hospitals through benefit concerts in major concert venues; (516) 621-0790.

Girl Scouts of the USA http://www.girlscouts.org/
Boy Scouts of America http://scouting.org/
The sites will help you find a Scout council near you. They also offer online games and activities.

National 4-H Council http://www.Fourhcouncil.edu
4-H programs and activities are focused on leadership, citizenship, and life skills. Members can attend clubs, camps, or after-school programs.

Ryan's Well Foundation http://www.ryanswell.ca
A nonprofit organization based in Ontario, Canada, dedicated to raising money to supply developing countries with clean drinking water; (613) 258-6832.

DOING THE RIGHT THING!

Search words: *hero, values, ideals*

Free The Children http://www.freethechildren.org
The largest network of children helping children in the world; FTC sponsors education and development programs in 45 countries. The international office is in Toronto, Ontario; (416) 925-5894.

The Giraffe Heroes Project http://www.giraffe.org
This web site inspires people to "stick their necks out" for the common good and profiles Giraffe heroes from around the world.

Idealist.org: Action Without Borders http://idealist.org/kt/index.html
Click on *Organizations started by Kids* to see what young people like you have accomplished in their communities.

My Hero http://www.myhero.com
The My Hero site posts thousands of stories of remarkable heroes, both adults and young people.

GOING AFTER KNOWLEDGE!

Search words: topics of interest; names of museums; *homework help*

Ask for Kids http://www.Askforkids.com
CyberSleuth Kids http://www.cybersleuth-kids.com
Ithaki for kids http://www.kids.ithaki.net
Encarta http://www.Encarta.msn.com
KidsClick! http://sunsite.berkeley.edu/KidsClick!
Yahooligans! the Web Guide for Kids http://www.Yahooligans.com
These powerful kid-friendly search engines find answers to your toughest questions and offer access to online encyclopedias and many other research and information tools.

The Children's Literature Web Guide
http://www.ucalgary.ca/~dKbrown/awards.html
A comprehensive guide to award-winning English-language books for young people sponsored by the University of Calgary.

Infoplease Homework Center http://www.infoplease.com/homework
Here is access to almanacs, encyclopedias, dictionaries, and more, including flashcards, learning quizzes, and games.

The JASON Project http://www.jason.org
A nonprofit organization that inspires learning in science, math, and technology through hands-on scientific discovery; (888) 527-6600.

Smithsonian Education
http://www.smithsonianeducation.org/students
Resources for students, families, and educators. The online IdeaLabs simulate a visit to one of the Smithsonian Institution's many museums in Washington, D.C.

World Wide Web Consortium http://www.w3.org/People/Berners-Lee/
Visit this site to learn more about Tim Berners-Lee and the Web; click on *Kids Questions* to read his answers to questions from young people.

JOINING TOGETHER!

Search words: *volunteer, teamwork, make a difference*

blogging. Search online under *blog hosts* to find sites such as http://www.blogger.com. Search under *blog templates* for design ideas.

Do Something: Young People Changing Our World
http://www.dosomething.org
This site inspires, supports, and celebrates young people changing themselves and our world.

foreign language phrases. Search online under *language translation.* You'll find sites such as http://www.google.com/language_tools, where you can translate words and phrases from one language to another.

international recipes. Search online under *international recipes.* You'll find sites such as http://www.internationalrecipes.net/recipes/, with recipes from all over the world.

The King Center http://www.thekingcenter.org
The official memorial to the legacy of Dr. Martin Luther King, Jr., helps you find community service opportunities near your home; (404) 526-8900.

Viet Nam Youth Projects http://www.vnyouthprojects.net
These two organizations raise and distribute funds to assist communities in Vietnam and to promote cultural exchange between Vietnam and the U.S.
Viet Nam Health, Education, and Literacy Projects (VNHELP)
http://www.vnhelp.org/

World Pen Pals http://www.world-pen-pals.com
This site promotes international friendship and cultural understanding by providing access to pen pals all over the world.

Index

More Good Books from Williamson

Welcome to Williamson Books! Our titles are available from your bookseller or directly from Williamson Books at Ideals Publications. Please see the next page for ordering information or to visit our web site. Thank you.

All books are suitable for children ages 7 through 14, and are 128 to 160 pages,
11 x 8½, $12.95, unless otherwise noted.

Benjamin Franklin Best Juvenile Nonfiction Award
Learning® Magazine Teachers' Choice Award
Oppenheim Toy Portfolio Best Book Award
SUPER SCIENCE CONCOCTIONS
50 Mysterious Mixtures for Fabulous Fun

Parents' Choice Honor Award
American Institute of Physics Science Writing Award
GIZMOS & GADGETS
Creating Science Contraptions that Work (& Knowing Why)

American Bookseller Pick of the Lists
Dr. Toy Best Vacation Product
KIDS' CRAZY ART CONCOCTIONS
50 Mysterious Mixtures for Art & Craft Fun

Little Hands® **series, ages 3 to 7, 10 x 8, 112 to 144 pages**

Early Childhood News Directors' Choice Award
Parent's Choice Approved
American Institute of Physics Science Writing Award
SCIENCE PLAY!
Beginning Discoveries for 2- to 6-Year-Olds

KINDERGARTEN SUCCESS
Helping Children Excel Right from the Start

Parents' Choice Recommended
EASY ART FUN!
Do-It-Yourself Crafts for Beginning Readers

LITTLE HANDS® **CELEBRATE AMERICA!**
Learning about the U.S.A. through Crafts and Activities

WOW! I'M READING!
Fun Activities to Make Reading Happen

KIDS WRITE!
Fantasy & Sci Fi, Mystery, Autobiography, Adventure & More!
by Rebecca Olien **Full color**

WORDPLAY CAFÉ
Cool Codes, Priceless Punzles® & Phantastic Phonetic Phun
Written and illustrated **Full color**
by Michael Kline

Parents' Choice Silver Honor Award
AWESOME OCEAN SCIENCE!
Investigating the Secrets of the Underwater World
by Cindy A. Littlefield

USING COLOR IN YOUR ART!
Choosing Colors for Impact & Pizzazz
by Sandi Henry **Full color**

Parents' Choice Recommended
Orbus Pictus Award for Outstanding Nonfiction
KIDS' ART WORKS!
Creating with Color, Design, Texture & More
by Sandi Henry

The Kids' Book of INCREDIBLY FUN CRAFTS
by Roberta Gould

Teachers' Choice Award
Dr. Toy Best Vacation Product
CUT-PAPER PLAY!
Dazzling Creations from Construction Paper
by Sandi Henry

Parents' Choice Approved Award
THE KIDS' MULTICULTURAL CRAFT BOOK
35 Crafts from Around the World
by Roberta Gould

Parents' Choice Gold Award
American Bookseller Pick of the Lists
THE KIDS' MULTICULTURAL ART BOOK
Art & Craft Experiences from Around the World
by Alexandra Michaels Terzian

Parents' Choice Recommended
ForeWord Magazine Book of the Year Finalist
PAPER-FOLDING FUN!
50 Awesome Crafts to Weave, Twist & Curl
by Ginger Johnson

JAZZY JEWELRY
Power Beads, Crystals, Chokers, & Illusion and Tattoo Styles
by Diane Baker

THE SECRET LIFE OF MATH
Discovering how (& why) numbers have survived from the cave dwellers to us!
by Ann McCallum **Full color**

Parents' Choice Approved
KIDS CREATE!
Art & Craft Experiences for 3- to 9-Year-Olds
by Laurie Carlson

Parents' Choice Recommended
The Kids' Guide to MAKING SCRAPBOOKS & PHOTO ALBUMS!
How to Collect, Design, Assemble, Decorate
by Laura Check

Selection of Book-of-the-Month; Scholastic Book Clubs
KIDS COOK!
Fabulous Food for the Whole Family
by Sarah Williamson and Zachary Williamson

Parents' Choice Approved
GREAT GAMES!
Old & New, Indoor/Outdoor, Travel, Board, Ball & Word
by Sam Taggar

Parents' Choice Recommended
KIDS' EASY-TO-CREATE WILDLIFE HABITATS
for small spaces in city, suburbs, countryside
by Emily Stetson

American Bookseller Pick of the Lists
Parents' Choice Approved
SUMMER FUN!
60 Activities for a Kid-Perfect Summer
by Susan Williamson

FIZZ, BUBBLE & FLASH!
Element Explorations & Atom Adventures for Hands-On Science Fun!
by Anita Brandolini, Ph.D.

Parents' Choice Gold Award
Benjamin Franklin Best Juvenile Nonfiction Award
KIDS MAKE MUSIC!
Clapping and Tapping from Bach to Rock
by Avery Hart and Paul Mantell

Parents' Choice Approved
Dr. Toy Best Vacation Product
KIDS GARDEN!
The Anytime, Anyplace Guide to Sowing & Growing Fun
by Avery Hart and Paul Mantell

Parents' Choice Recommended
Children's Digest Health Education Award
The Kids' Guide to FIRST AID
All about Bruises, Burns, Stings, Sprains & Other Ouches
by Karen Buhler Gale, R.N.

American Bookseller Pick of the Lists
Parents' Choice Recommended
ADVENTURES IN ART
Arts & Crafts Experiences for 8- to 13-Year-Olds
by Susan Milord

American Bookseller Pick of the Lists
Skipping Stones Nature & Ecology Honor Award
ECOART!
Earth-Friendly Art & Craft Experiences for 3- to 9-Year-Olds
by Laurie Carlson

Benjamin Franklin Best Education/Teaching Gold Award
Parent's Guide Children's Media Award
HAND-PRINT ANIMAL ART
by Carolyn Carreiro, full color, $14.95

Parents' Choice Approved
Benjamin Franklin Best Multicultural Book Award
THE KIDS' MULTICULTURAL COOKBOOK
Food & Fun Around the World
by Deanna F. Cook

Visit Our Web site!

To see what's new at Williamson and learn more about specific books, visit our secure web site at:

www.williamsonbooks.com
or www.Idealsbooks.com